A TIME TO MOURN
& A TIME TO DANCE

A TIME TO MOURN & A TIME TO DANCE

A PILGRIMAGE FROM DEATH TO FULL LIFE

LEE ANNE MORGAN

Hudson River Valley

Copyright © 2019 by Lee Anne Morgan

All rights reserved. No part of this publication may be reproduced, distributed or transmitted in any form or by any means, including photocopying, recording, digital scanning, or other electronic or mechanical methods, without the prior written permission of the publisher, except in the case of brief quotations embodied in critical reviews and certain other noncommercial uses permitted by copyright law. For permission requests, please address FullLife Publishing.

Published 2019
Printed in the United States of America
ISBN-13: 978-0-578-50674-6

www.timetomourntimetodance.com

Scripture quotations are from the ESV® Bible (The Holy Bible, English Standard Version®), copyright© 2001 by Crossway, a publishing ministry of Good News Publishers. Used by permission. All rights reserved. Lyrics from song, *So Will I*, are by Hillsong United Worship, Sydney, Australia.

Front cover photo by Lee Anne Morgan
Text design by Elizabeth Cline

Content

Author's Note	ix
2018 - Prologue	1
2003 - Fifteen Years Earlier	5
2004	55
2005	135
2018 - Reprise	147
Acknowledgements	167

For everything there is a season,
and a time for every matter under heaven:

a time to weep, and a time to laugh;
a time to mourn, and a time to dance;

Ecclesiastes 3:4

Dedication

This book is dedicated to Lily, my lost sister-of-the-womb. And, to all the unborn children who were and are deprived of a voice, a soul, a name—and of life and love.

Author's Note

To all those who have gone before me seeking *The Way, The Truth, and The Life* and found the Living Waters, I thank you for your courage, blessings, and revelations. And, to all who are lost and bewildered in our broken, fallen world, know that I share my own story to inspire hope and the healing of souls. May this testimony be a raft, a boat, a bridge across your calm and troubled waters. *A Time to Mourn & A Time to Dance* was written for you wherever you are in your life's journey.

I offer my deepest gratitude, in His name, for *all* that unfolded in the miracle of my life.

2018

For I have learned in whatever situation I am to be content. I know how to be brought low, and I know how to abound. In any and every circumstance, I have learned the secret of facing plenty and hunger, abundance and need. I can do all things through Him who strengthens me.

~ Philippians 4:11-13

Prologue

It is 4:30 A.M. on this still, sultry August morning. The temperatures will reach the mid-nineties. This is not an unusual time for me to be awake. Morning rituals unfold as I brew a pot of Assam tea. I listen to the first bird's morning praise greeting dawn's hazy light on the horizon. An open book rests on my lap.

I forgot that today is my seventy-fifth birthday. Three-quarters of a century! What is next? I don't know. I surrendered expectations for the future several years ago for they no longer hold any lure for me. Nevertheless, I do want to tell you a story.

It's an authentic account, and it is mine. Each narrative's tapestry presents distinctive strands of emotional and physical textures and colors. Some, strong and bold, others fragile and subtle, illumine the pathways and mysteries of one's life. It is not without apprehension I walk into the tapestry of my life. I search for a starting point, a critical time or circumstance, that forms the genesis of the story I want to share with you.

Grainy images flash before me like an old film projector flickering, skipping frames every so often. A bottle of Shalimar perfume. Fever. Drugs. A leg brace and wheelchair. An old black man in Georgia and an angel at sunrise. Long-stemmed roses in glossy white boxes wrapped in red satin bows. Flawlessly applied small rouge circles on sixteen faces. Blue Highways with pink elephants. Jackie Gleason and June Taylor. Tony Bennett, Glenn Miller, and Tommy Dorsey. Dom DeLuise, Lee Remick, Kevin McCarthy, and more. Stories written. Stories burned. A remote cabin with galloping horses. Beloved animals and supernatural creatures. Love and loss. Mourning and joy. Only one image remains steady as the fragmented images jump and change: A cross on a hill with crimson stains.

I am the only person left who knows what happened. A life was eliminated at the beginning. Four others directly involved died long ago. I seek the truth regarding events in my life—some beyond the reach of comprehension. If I uncover the facts, perhaps the final threads will entwine together with surety, ensuring no loose ends, no unraveling. Closure.

Living seven decades is not particularly noteworthy, yet one strand of my personal tapestry is: *I was nearly never born.* This is one reason, though there are others, I try to understand what is and what was and to accept that which must remain at the edge of mystery.

So, I write. And as I write, I remember.

2003
15 Years Earlier

Upon You I have leaned from before my birth;
You are He who took me from my mother's womb.

~Psalm 71:6

August 25

In a place and time long forgotten by me, I read we are all *athletes of God* in some area of our lives. Is this the strand unique to each of us? The marrow of our very existence we seek to discover? And did God plant it there? Using a fountain pen filled with the emerald green ink I prefer, I write these thoughts in a weathered, brown leather journal to explore and record emotions and details of my external and internal worlds.

After decades, my heart still feels sadness of almost not living this life. The attempted erasure of my existence is not new information. However, I believe my melancholy is related to something I've yet to confront and reconcile, something I'm pushing away. Nonetheless, before my story is complete, the final word written, I would like to understand *why I was saved*.

Henry will arrive soon for his saucer of milk. I set the kettle on the stove for my pot of Assam tea. Upon his arrival, Henry sits on our porch with eyes fixed on the oval glass window of our home's entrance door, anticipating my footsteps and the turn of the well-worn, egg-shaped brass handle. Henry is a large orange and brown tiger-striped tabby with otherworldly eyes. In full sun, they appear to be pure gold like that of a mysterious, mythical creature, but they are merely generously flecked with amber, inhabiting deep brown irises. He is large yet sinewy, a work of art that moves and does so with the grace and ferocity of a Bengal tiger. Though Henry climbs trees, hunts, and gets into skirmishes I choose not to think about, he returns faithfully at this hour every morning.

Henry and I live on a mountaintop in a log cabin, my home and sanctuary. The cabin was a fiftieth birthday present I decided to give myself ten years ago. This morning brings a chill to the air announcing the first hint of autumn. I am high enough on this mountain to witness the lush green leaves transform into dazzling color. Hues of red, yellow, gold, and bright orange will explode across this mountain and those surrounding us in a few short weeks.

While I wait for Henry's arrival and the kettle to boil, I regard the decor and design of the cabin, which was my canvas, obsession too, when I first took ownership. There is beauty in every corner and angle of the Great Room, the blending of warm rusticity with contemporary elegance. Though the basic cabin was here, I invested many months and far too much money not only in the interior design and decor but also in the exterior landscaping. The road and the land leading to the cabin were rocks and mud and woodland when I first arrived. As I drove the one-mile long steep, muddy road to see the dwelling and stepped over the threshold of its entrance, I was captivated by its space and light. I asked the owner how much he wanted for a binder. We closed three weeks later.

The Great Room where I spend most of my days living and writing is open space, one-and-a-half stories high with cathedral ceilings and hand-hewn pine beams. The room, a generous size, embraces the living and dining areas, the kitchen, and my writing desk. The walls are the inside of the exterior logs of the cabin. Mullioned casement windows and skylights are plentiful throughout, allowing light to flow in from all directions.

The furniture, Shabby-Chic and comfortable in soft earth tones, surrounds a large, red Vermont Castings wood stove. The stove's pipe makes its own artistic statement. It is a flawless, vertical black cylinder, a perfect spire rising one-and-a-half stories.

A late-1700s rectangular pine dining table with bench seating, denoting a preferred communal-style for breaking bread, dwells under a small crystal chandelier near a high-tech kitchen of stainless steel and black granite. Odd and impractical for a log cabin. Peaceful and beautiful to me.

Henry arrives just as my tea is fully brewed. I splash cream into my mug before pouring the tea, and then present Henry with his saucer of milk. I observe how methodical he is consuming the liquid. He is slow and intent in a feline form of meditation. Lick. Lick. Pause. Lick. Lick. Pause. His rhythm is constant, not one beat is missed. Lick. Lick. Pause.

Henry finishes his milk as I pour my second mug of tea. We walk toward my writing space, a sweeping oval mahogany partner's desk identical on both sides. I am grateful for this massive expanse in which to spread papers and write. And so is Henry. He sits like a Sphinx staring out the window perhaps recalling his nighttime adventures. He finally curls up for his morning nap with a loud, satisfied purr.

I look through the windows in front of my desk as the sun begins its ascent in swathes of soft shades of lavender, pale orange, and pink. I stroke Henry as I sip my tea. I lean in close before losing myself to the journal and observe my boy in slumber. I've photographed the details of my feline companion many times, focusing on his long, thick, white whiskers and short, sleek-to-the-muscle fur, pure white feathered tufts sprouting well above the tips of his ears, an apricot-pink nose, and the black-as-pitch pads of his large, sturdy paws. This moment is not negotiable. It is perfect in its simplicity. I uncap my fountain pen and listen to the sound of paper as the pen's nib lays down its green ink, a prelude for beginning my initial musings and writing for the day.

People describe my home as a storybook cabin-in-the-woods, a haven, even heaven-on-earth. They are right. It is all of these and more. This homestead is not unlike a cherished being. I've shared some details with you hoping to brand them into your mind. What people do not see is the subtle, stealthy fear hovering over my soul that this safe harbor, this sacred home will perish. I keep the darkness of this thought tightly swaddled within, but there are moments when it roars into my heart and spirit declaring tragedy, sadness, loss. I do not know if this is prophetic thought, or a lack of faith in the good fortune given to me in this life.

Friends and associates do not suspect this hidden fear exists unless I share it, and only one close friend is aware of this restlessness in my soul. She is the one who noticed the absence of anything denoting family, or childhood. However, residing on shelves and tabletops and my desk, there are books, small sculptures, and hand-crafted items intermingled with carefully selected sea shells from an extended visit on an empty beach. Nonetheless, the shroud of unease of losing this refuge has no threads to weave into this narrative's tapestry. No, this fear is merely an unfortunate haunting, an unwanted dream.

August 26

 I promised you an honest tale. There were so many beginnings and endings in my life. Choices made and not made, paths walked and others not, doors opened and closed, life lived, and phenomena ignored. Even so, let us begin now! I will tell you about my walking stick. It is an ideal place to start for this stick is like no other. It is a snake stick relating to yesterday as well as the present, and possibly tomorrow.

 I walk most days even in winter. This unique walking stick is hand-carved from ironwood by a mountain man who once thought he was passing through but remained on this mountain. The stick is four-feet-eleven inches high when I hold it upright and it is carved, too realistically, in the pattern of a diamondback snake. The head of the snake is the top of the stick. The snake's head is in the process of swallowing a frog. I use this snake stick for there are loose rocks and slippery shale on these mountain paths explicitly forged for my use a decade ago. This mountaintop home is filled with beauty and mystery and wisdom under each rock, at the top of every tree, and in a single blade of grass.

 The longer I live here, the more I study the marvels of Creation. A small insect embarks on a journey in what appears to the human eye a circuitous route yet for the insect there is a goal. When my footstep strikes too close to a garden snake's shelter under a bush or rock, its instincts are to uncurl and slither smoothly, quickly to another secluded place. I witness the renewal of a winter-brown fern as it is born again into the new, fresh green of spring. And, looking high up, I observe a red tail hawk write her aria in the sky.

There are nature's scents too as I inhale the sweet-yet-pungent bouquet of fresh autumn leaves and the dry, crisp winter air as it invigorates my lungs. The clean scent of spring signals the restoration of life in the whole of nature, and the summer's warm rain nourishes the earth releasing its inherent muskiness. These are dense woods consisting of maple, oak, birch, and tall ancient hemlock trees. Nature takes a different form every day. No sunrise or sunset repeats itself, cloud formations weave their distinctive patterned language in the sky, and each mist dons a cloak of personality and mood as it glides through these soft-shouldered Catskill Mountains.

The cabin sits on forty-three acres, not unlike a preserve for wildlife. There are deer, wild turkey, pheasant, quail, grouse, bobcat, bear, red tail hawks, bald eagles, coyotes, and all the natural, and supernatural, beings who inhabit this mountain and its forest.

There is a barred owl that resides here with me. It is surprising I'm even aware of him since owls are nocturnal and not usually visible during the day. Moreover, their brown-black and gray-to-white plumage blend with tree bark so they are difficult to discern. Nonetheless, this owl sits on a tree limb outside my window boldly visible in the light of day. I named him Shakespeare. Owls are reserved creatures and do not openly present themselves to mere mortals. He frequently flies ahead of me from branch-to-limb during my daily walks. According to local Native Americans, it is a great honor for Shakespeare to accompany me.

He and Henry are born predators. When Shakespeare first made himself known to me, I was concerned. Though Henry is tall and muscular, Shakespeare is the dominant predator. It is my belief they made a covenant with one another. Or, it is my wishful thinking. Shakespeare never threatened Henry, and Henry accepted Shakespeare without a twitch of a whisker. I often watch Henry napping at the foot of a favorite perch of Shakespeare's, a low-hanging gnarled limb of an old oak tree. With his wide, soft, brown eyes including that slow, all-knowing barred-owl blink, he appears to observe me closely as I write.

I am a photographer, writer, and painter. It was not always this way. Consuming the first twenty years of my life, I danced and sang professionally. I took a twenty-year hiatus (if one is audacious enough to call twenty years a *pause*) from any kind of artistic pursuits for unabashed material gain in the advertising, marketing, and consulting arenas. And arenas they were. Following those years of worldliness and money, travel and a modicum of success, I now try to plunge fully into what I believe I've been given to do. Write and photograph and paint. I say 'try' because I still need to support myself. I do as little worldly-work possible. My camera, pen, journal, and my paints and brushes are the fundamental ingredients of my existence and equanimity.

I performed from the age of six through my mid-twenties. An interviewer from a local newspaper in Chicago asked me, "Why do you enjoy performing? The applause? The glamor?" He commented that it was clear to him I did. I replied, "While those things have their appeal, it is about communication for me. I feel a communion with the audience. I sense their heartbeats, their excitement keeping pace with my dance rhythms, and, yes, their exhilaration when I spin so fast my costume skirt whirls like a cyclone. Of course, the applause is nice to receive, but it is better to know there was a communion of souls. Mine to theirs and theirs to mine." A bit precious? Yes. I was sixteen at the time. However, it was and is to this day a sincere desire.

I am no longer a performance artist. I hope that the act of creating communication through words and images goes beyond my selfish indulgences. Many, though not all, artists are self-absorbed creatures. We are privileged to live lives of fantasy and dreams, but not without pain and sadness too. Yet we have the means to communicate with the world in exciting, evocative ways. We are never alone because our inner lives teem with imagination. If one image, or story I write, touches another soul, stirs insight and willingness to see the world through a different lens, then my work is meaningful. It may serve as a relevant, hopeful purpose for another. Idealistic? Yes, for some. Nonetheless, it is possible I can accomplish one small thing that is right and good.

August 27

 The realization it was time for me to confront a tragedy in my life started a few weeks ago when a friend mentioned my upcoming sixtieth birthday. We decided to have a celebration in my tepee, which resides behind the cabin. Rather than observe a milestone event, I thought a memorial service honoring the Water Child, a happening sixty years ago steeped in fact as well as enigma, would be a first step toward facing a wound that even now though healed remains tender.

 These two words, water and child, are translated from a Japanese ceremony, Mizuko kuyō, or *fetus memorial service*. Mizuko literally means child of water, child of the womb. And, yes, this tale undeniably begins with one who was truly a Water Child.

 The Water Child was my twin sister who shared my mother's womb with me for almost twenty weeks. I named her Lily. I considered the words 'water child' as a name for they are soft in tone and conjure a sense of grace and well-being. For my sister, however, they were anything but those things. While I was born on this day, Lily died a few months earlier. Sixty years later I continue to wonder how I managed to emerge into existence following her death. My sister's brief existence was never honored. It was held in secrecy for twenty-one years. And so, sister-of-the-womb, I honor you this day. There is a timeless quality to the name Lily, and most assuredly, my sister is a child-of-eternity.

I started the wood fire in the tepee two hours ago. By the time of arrival of two close friends, Anna and Peddler, the embers will be warm and glowing before the early autumn chill of evening wraps around us. There is a bottle of Pierre Ferrand Cognac for my friends, an indulgence I once loved too much. Today, in the left back pocket of my jeans, is a coin from Alcoholics Anonymous.

One of my friends, Anna Kaplan, was a former New York City executive for a Fortune 100 company. Today, she is a landscaper and has built a small coterie of loyal, appreciative clients. Anna gave up an extravagant life-style, and not a shabby small fortune, to come and live in this remote area of upstate New York. She not only gave it all up, but she literally gave her possessions and money away to charities and various foundations important to her heart. Moreover, she then gifted funds to strangers and families at homeless shelters.

Anna is five-feet eight inches tall and all muscle given her work. She is olive skinned with a face reflecting premature age-lines around her mouth and eyes given she is outdoors most of the time. Her hair is blue-black, parted in the center, and hangs in a perfect blunt cut to her waist. Anna's eyes are coal black. Her heart is as large as the sky and as pure as the first snow. She is forty-five years old and I am proud to call her friend.

My other companion, Peddler, is a sixty-four-year old mountain man and one of the last of his kind. Peddler carved my snake stick. He lives in a tepee most of the year. For those who have never seen him, he makes an unforgettable first impression. He is over six-feet tall with a white beard reaching his waist, which is neatly tied at the bottom with thin woven leather fringe. Peddler's thick white hair is worn in a long, low pony tail, or single braid, and he sports a weathered broad rimmed oilskin hat. His scent is of wood smoke from his tepee and forge fires. He is the soul of this mountain, and has been neither of, nor in, the worldly-world for many years.

Peddler knows these woods well and wears them. There are feathers, bones, teeth, and all kinds of talismans hanging from his neck, belt, wrists, and hair. He is a gentleman's hunter and has my permission to hunt this land. He uses bow and arrow and a muzzle-loading gun, so he only hunts during specific seasons. Peddler went to Harvard Medical School and practiced psychiatry for a dozen years, maybe more. One day he closed his office door, walked away, and never returned. He said, "I knew when I no longer cared about my patients that I needed to leave for their sake. I always preferred living outdoors and was a sportsman since boyhood. I am here now. I am home." Anna and Peddler moved out of their materialistic worlds. Neither is wealthy in what our world perceives as affluence. They are blessed with inner peace, and an ease of living that goes beyond substantial monetary gain.

Ah, but I still cling to a few sophisticated ways. This cabin and land and having the money to sustain it is but one of several indulgences I enjoy. Though my wants have diminished these past several years, there were many more at one time. I flirt with the idea and courage of Anna and Peddler to willingly walk off a cliff and free myself of worldly attachments.

No matter how perfect my life appears to others, it is linked to a form of enslavement. Material well-being is yoked to servitude to maintain survival in a worldly-world. How we define servitude is a debate-of-debates. However, as this story unfolds, my testimony sheds a bright light on serving a materialistic world. I've admitted to anxiety that this sanctuary, my Camelot, could perish. This is driven by fear. My foreboding is more profound than the cabin and land. It is about not having enough. What I know is that I am not ready to walk off the cliff for I dread I will not find freedom but deprivation and a depth of suffering from which I would never recover.

Peddler, Anna, and I assemble at the tepee's entrance. Henry paces outside. Shakespeare sits on the safest limb closest to the tepee. Darkness arrives, and we are silent for a few moments listening to nighttime come to life in the sounds of the forest.

Lily's ceremony begins as I pour the amber colored Cognac into the large, delicate brandy snifters, and green tea in a mug for myself. We drink a toast to her lost life here on earth. As a Christian, I should believe I will see her again in heaven. I collect bibles more for their literary styles than a commitment to God, faith, or religion. At best, I consider myself a liberal Christian.

Anna begins smudging sage and sweet-grass while chanting in a Native American tongue I believe is Haudenosaunee, commonly known as Iroquois. While she continues her low, soft chant, I recite from The Book of Job, 1.21, *"Naked I came from my mother's womb, and naked shall I return. The LORD gave, and the LORD has taken away; blessed be the name of the LORD."*

Peddler plays his guitar as unfamiliar yet soothing melodies float into the night. Anna and I sit back on large tree stumps wrapped in woolen blankets for cushioning, and absorb the scents, the music, and our drinks. We are silent for a few minutes listening to the insects, hoots, and the call of a coyote. Henry's shadow circles the tepee until he is satisfied. He finally enters and graces us with his presence, settling next to me for a stroke of his ears. I hear Shakespeare vocalize the unique barred owl call only once perhaps to honor Lily, my hidden and forgotten sister. No longer, though, for she is now remembered.

August 28

 I sip tea while Henry enjoys his snooze. Shakespeare sits on a branch peering at me, occasionally punctuating the silence with his nine-note call, *who cooks for you, who cooks for you all?*

 Lily's memorial service did not soothe my heart. I did what I believed was right, even though it was sixty years too late. Despite this disquietude, I continue with my narrative facing THE EMPTY PAGE. I struggle with the disclosure of the truth. It is raw and harsh yet remains surreal to me. But before I reveal anything more, there are events in my life you should know that shaped my choices and who I am today. Though I live in voluntary solitude, it was not always this way. I've shared details about this cabin, nature's cathedral surrounding it, and some aspects of my life here. However, I would be remiss if I didn't tell you about the horse barn down the hill from the cabin. And Dave.

 The barn is a vital part of this land—a privileged life experience woven with love into my tapestry. The barn's inception, the horses and the mingled scent of hay and manure and soft muzzles, lead to recollections of love and a large life. The happenings and the memories are mixed with joy and mourning in equal proportion.

What a *frisson* to ride and gallop through meadows and unfettered dirt roads! Six horses, not all mine, were stabled in the barn at one point. Dave built the barn a year after I moved here. He also cleared the land and forged the trails for walking and riding through this mountain's forest. The horses are gone now. I miss their whinnying in the mornings when Dave came to put them out to pasture tossing their hay. Dave is gone too. In fact, all the men whom I loved, except for one, have died.

Dave Dixon stepped on to my cabin's porch during my first week of living here, shook my hand saying, "Ma'am, it sure looks like you need a road." It was the warmth, the firm grip of his calloused hand when I knew something in my life was about to shift. While shaking his hand, I scanned sky-blue eyes, a weathered, tan face with deep inset lines, especially when he smiled, and silver hair sparkling in the dazzling sunshine on that first warm April day. Yes, I needed a road, clearing of land, landscaping, stone walls, and much more. We talked the afternoon away, made plans, and realized within a few weeks how in love we were.

Dave and I never married, yet it was a steadfast union of love. Laughter was abundant, though we had serious debates and sometimes heated arguments. Nonetheless, we respected our differences and expressed them in truths-well-told. Our time together publicly and privately was expressed in a depth of patience, tenderness, and abiding love. I formally married three good, fine men, but I miss the authenticity of Dave. There was sweetness to our seasons together. We were equally yoked.

Dave brought playfulness into my oh-so-serious life with people, family, motorcycle rides, eating ice cream, and even a Big Mac with fries instead of my lean, tasteless macrobiotic diet. He taught me to ride horses, especially the one he said was born for me. Bubba was his name and an un-stately one at that for a noble spotted Tennessee Walking horse standing fifteen hands.

If you don't know this breed, the Tennessee Walker is known for its unique gait. It is a smooth four-beat running-walk with flashy movement. Bubba was a three-and-a-half-year-old gelding and I was an inexperienced rider. Dave was right, though. Bubba was sweet, patient-yet-spirited, and smooth-gaited. And critical to my lack of riding experience, he was sure-footed and bomb proof. Bubba was sensitive to the reins and my legs. He required only a delicate nudge from me.

Dave and I groomed all six horses, fed and watered and walked them too. On a bright, cold winter's night after feeding carrots to the six large heads poking out of their stalls, feeling the soft muzzles gently inhale the sweetness from our hands, we walked up the hill to the cabin through crunchy, packed snow. Dave pointed to the mass of sparkling stars, an audacious extravaganza for there was no ambient light to diminish their brilliance. He wrapped his arm tightly around my shoulder and pulled me into his chest whispering, "Do you see those stars? That is God. No church walls. No dogma." Though not religious on any level, Dave saw the Creator in everything. His eyes shimmered with the light of heaven, at least to me. My heart still aches for Dave's touch and warmth. I miss you, Dave.

Oh, how I miss you.

As I think back upon three formal marriages, I treasure enduring gifts from each. Oh, there were the usual presents of jewelry, perfume, and flowers. Yet one lengthy white box filled with gardenias, my favorite flower, stands out from the rest. It was a 50th birthday present from my second husband. What I cherish from each marriage, subtler and more indirect than baubles and stuff, may appear simple to most. However, they enabled decisions and created pathways in my life, enriching it with time.

My first husband, Tom, gave me an appreciation for movies, screenplays, directorial techniques, and music of all genres. He was an avid reader and introduced me to James Agee and Walker Evans in their seminal work, *Let Us Now Praise Famous Men*. There wasn't a glimmer of foresight that this one book would lead me to my own form of photojournalism decades later through a blog, enabling me to combine my photography, paintings, and writing. We divorced after an eleven-year marriage.

Arthur Allan Anderson was my second husband. Arthur remains my dear friend to this day. He has witnessed the seasons-of-my-heart through our years as husband and wife, business partners, and now as loving, good friends. He is a touchstone of constancy that I hold dear in an upside-down world. Though not a man of faith in the traditional religions-of-the-world, he is most assuredly a man of his own brand of faith. He gives often to others with total abandonment, crossed continents for a friend in trouble, and is generous with his money and his time. He is a creative and skilled businessman, wise with money, a lover of nature and art, and loyal. While he taught me to be a savvy businesswoman, he helped me to see the critical importance of being true to my heart. Before you think it, I will say it: True to my heart is trite. Until recently though, it was an arduous climb up Mt. Everest for me. Yet Arthur supported my every step, every move on to a new path and still does. We also divorced after eleven years.

Jerry was my third, and last, husband. I was attracted to his brilliance. Both sides of his brain were in high gear. He was creative as a writer and photographer, and extremely adept in the early-on experimental science of computer technology. Jerry is the one who placed a camera in my hands. Unknown to me then, my career as a photographer began. He presented me with a small Minolta point-and-shoot for one of my birthdays.

We walked through Battery Park, close to where we lived in New York City, to inaugurate my new camera, and I shot several rolls of film. This was the pre-digital era, so the film required development. While I forgot about that afternoon, a few days later Jerry arrived home saying, "Do you want to see the photos we took?" Assuming he had taken stunning shots from our Battery Park foray, I was ready. He proceeded to lay one image at a time across our table and said, "I believe you have a photographer's eye." And to my surprise, I agreed. My world shifted in those brief moments, though I had no idea the immensity of change about to happen. My divorce with Jerry was not as amicable as with Tom and Arthur. Our marriage lasted a mere two years. (Jerry died during the final months of writing this narrative. Oh, how much he wanted to read the draft. But his cancer caused horrific suffering in its final stage, and he could no longer focus. Jerry emailed me several times and I thanked him for buying my first camera. We managed, though, to heal the wounds between us.)

Three failed marriages? I was needy. I set high expectations for others and, of course, myself. Neediness and setting impossible goals for perfection was an emotional blueprint for failure. I fell in love deeply and fast. I could've been the poster-woman for *Love Is Blind*. I loved loving but surrendered too much of my soul in each marriage. I did not know how to ask for what I needed. None of my husbands, and indeed not Dave, expected me to relinquish my needs and desires. Yet I was afraid to ask, or to say no, or to pursue an interest not to their liking due to my insecure, fabricated fear they would leave. I was terrified of not having someone to love and being unloved and alone. Abandoned. And there it is. My sister left me alone in the womb, though surely not her choice. Even so, there is an ephemeral shadow memory of being close, united, and then torn apart. I perpetuated that experience in my life at least three times with husbands and many more times in other ways.

October 1

The leaves are in full pageantry. I never weary of bearing witness to the changing seasons. Autumn is remarkable here. Color is displayed across the mountains no matter where I turn in the three-hundred-sixty-degree view. The cabin's sweet aromatic wood smoke scents the air creating a haven of hearth and home and warmth. Fallen leaves crunch under my feet as I finish my walk for the day. Henry suns himself on the porch steps and follows me into the cabin. I place the snake stick against the doorjamb and put on a kettle for tea. While waiting, I check my email and see one from Anna. "Lee Anne, how about some chili sans meat tonight? I'll bring bread and salad." Umm. I was planning to sink into my sofa in front of a blazing wood fire and begin the second reading of Agatha Christie's, *The Murder of Roger Ackroyd*.

This is when my preference for seclusion butts up against being with my good friend. I reply, "Great! Let's make it early around five-thirty?" Anna already knew I made veggie chili earlier in the week and it is better now with the rich spices thoroughly merged, so there's little for me to do.

My tea is ready. I stoke the stove, add two smaller logs, and finally sink into the down feathered cushions of the sofa while Henry sits on its broad, plush arm next to me. I hold my hot mug of tea in both hands studying the flames flickering from one log soaring to another and then another until with great crescendo there is a blazing fire. I reluctantly get up and walk over to the desk to jot down some notes and assess my feelings about not writing for six weeks. I know the subject matter I want to write, but depression descends upon me when I am bereft of even one word.

I look in the mirror and see a five-foot-three slender woman with green eyes and a short crop of salt and pepper hair chopped and spiked going in all directions. I like it. It's wild and messy. I've always been fashionable if not utterly 'done.' Nails, hair, makeup, and designer suits as if I stepped out of *Vogue*. Only a few of those items remain in my closet for select consulting projects I'm obligated to perform to support my home and whimsies.

Anna and I spent the evening eating and drinking tea, talking about our love lives or lack thereof, our futures, our health, our spiritual well-being. I had so little to say about my personal form of spirituality. I recently described myself as a Christian-Buddhist, an oxymoron. Anna is very comfortable in her Native American ways and beliefs. I respect her convictions, though I wrestle with her view of God. She does not believe in a triune Godhead, but neither does she honor pagan statues and rituals. Anna believes in one God, the Great Spirit, rather than a Trinity. She also believes this one God is more significant than we realize as He is the Creator of the universe. I was raised to believe in the Father, the Son, and the Holy Spirit. It is complicated for me. Not God per se, but the religiosity surrounding Him. Nevertheless, I own several Bibles of different translations, each one open to some section of its sixty-six books. I feel compelled to read them. I tell myself it is for research and literary reasons. Anna says, "They are calling to you, so pay attention." I wonder.

My present dilemma, however, is not my collection of Bibles. It is that I've gone dry in my writing. To move forward, I must return to the events that were once my life.

October 2

Shakespeare sits on his personal branch of the oak tree and stares at me. I feel his reprimand for delaying what I need to do. I peer back into his large round eyes, so calm, yet all-knowing. *Do not condemn me Shakespeare! Lead me out of my self-created wilderness.*

A large mug of freshly brewed tea sits next to my notes. I had a fitful sleep tossing and turning all night. I felt like Jacob wrestling with the Angel of the LORD. Unlike Jacob, I didn't receive any guidance, nor blessing, on how to write the truth of what happened to my sister and me. I hold back, in part, wondering if anyone cares to know. Or is it something I should place into an electronic Zip file and bury into the deepest folds of my memories? *No.* I need to write about what happened. And, though I'll never have all the facts, I possess a few critical details.

I still can't grasp Lily's death and the fact I exist, for this was no miscarriage. It was premeditated murder. My parents' intent was to destroy life.

No one suspected my mother carried twins. How did the doctor not hear two hearts beat? There were only backroom abortions performed in 1943. World War II was in full operation, and many women who had abortions were losing husbands to war. My father was unable to serve in the military for he had a small deformity in one foot. Yet he held a civil service position as a fireman, so my parents were together and not separated as were military wives and husbands. I do not judge the women who aborted their children during wartime years. However, I am haunted by questions: How did they eventually feel about their decisions? Were they troubled with regret? Shame? Relief? And, as the years rolled forward, would they have made a different choice if they could undo what was done?

My parents' reasons for wanting to abort their child was that my father felt he and mom could not afford a baby, though dad's income as a fireman, a civil servant, was assured. Though they were not poor, money was the impetus for killing the life in my mother's womb.

In my mother's time, abortions were illegal yet performed. Doctors used long steel rods of some sort to clean out the womb. Women often took medicines to enable miscarriage rather than undergo an invasive procedure. Sometimes they did both. Lily's life ended late in my mother's second trimester. After slipping through my mother's womb, it was apparent Lily was a fully formed female baby. My maternal grandmother, whom I eventually called Granny, picked Lily out of the bloody mess to examine her, perhaps checking for any sign of life. Lily was dead, so Granny flushed my sister down the toilet. My grandmother, mother, and father believed the act was complete.

My family was Roman Catholic. That they did not bury and memorialize Lily is incomprehensible to me. Almost unforgivable. What were the conditions of their hearts and souls regarding the sanctity of life, a precept observed in most enduring religions?

I believe the universe shifts ever so subtly when one single life is silenced through violence. Whether we choose to acknowledge this or not, today's groaning, fallen world is evidence of our popular interest in the small self. Rather than preserving human life and the resources of our planet, standing steadfast against violence and terror, providing support for those who are victims, marginalized, or just forgotten, too many self-appointed deities summarily dismiss these issues or avert their eyes entirely. I too have looked the other way. I confess I have not done enough. My soul is restless, and it is telling me that the lack of compassion nor taking substantive action must change.

Immediate consequences followed my parents' decision. Though my presence was still unknown to them and would remain so for another two months, my mother almost died while I was in her womb. She developed peritonitis, a dangerous form of blood poisoning that originates in the abdomen from infection often caused by trauma. It was only a few short years later that more serious repercussions of Lily's death and my birth emerged into my parents' lives.

And in mine.

October 6

It is 2 A.M. Some being cries out, again and again, a haunting, terrifying lament. I believed I was dreaming. Yet this is real and unending, and I'm unsettled. The veil between rational and supernatural worlds is thin. During what I thought was a dream, I believed it was the cry of a child. A very young child, but not a baby. Now I realize there is a raw, painful wail coming from the forest surrounding my cabin. I sit and listen, trying to discern the nature of the sound. I determine it is an animal, not a child, in great distress. Perhaps a mating cry? Or, a requiem for the dead? Henry is still outside, and I wonder if he is hurt, or caught something, causing himself or his prey pain and suffering. I walk to my bedroom's sliding glass doors that open to a deck. I stand there in the brisk night air trying to locate the mystery. I see nothing, yet the sound is eerily close. I stop searching the forest floor for movement and look up through the trees where a full moon shines a harsh light across the landscape. If there were music, it would be devoid of harmony, possessing a sole dissonance with a macabre undertone.

Without warning on this still, cold night, the wind suddenly whirls around the cabin and me. I stand still watching the frenzy transform gnarled tree limbs and slender branches into an eerie balletic flow of night dancers. The boughs, even smaller trunks, lean to one side and then the other, stretching toward yet another bending tree. There is no beauty in this ballet, but, rather, sinister and bony skeletons performing a menacing dance. Then, all sound, all movement stops. No wind. No wailing. Only silence. The trees stand motionless. The experience is unearthly if not wholly mystical. An ominous full moon, nighttime wind-dancers-cum-skeletons, and an unknown being crying a requiem before moonlight becomes daylight. I walk back to the sliding doors of the bedroom, paused, then look over my shoulder, uttering in a low, raspy voice I do not recognize as my own. "Go away. *Go away.*"

I leave the comfort of my bedroom with its subtle butter-cream tones on the walls and carpeted floors, a spacious bed stacked with down-feathered pillows, a gas-log soapstone stove, and a luxurious down comforter. I slide the French pocket doors into the thick log walls. They represent a portal from one area of my life to another. This night I need a clear vision of space and leave them open.

I stoke the thick bed of coals in the living room wood stove and stack a combination of large ash and fragrant Applewood into the stove. The fire climbs as flames rapidly consume the layers of wood. And, it is a blessed relief to be in the warmth of a roaring fire.

I pace and worry waiting for five o'clock to arrive. This is Henry's usual time to appear on the porch. I walk with trepidation to the door and finally find a full breath to exhale for there he sits perfectly whole, motionless, and unscathed from any fight. I am so grateful to see him. As I open the door, he walks with great composure to his saucer. Nothing is in it. He looks up at me, and I begin to pour cream rather than plain milk, my treat for his safe return. We both walk toward my desk, and I start writing this entry into my journal.

Nonetheless, I cannot forget the sound of the heart-rending wail, nor can I fathom the sudden wind or the performance of the skeletal tree dancers.

This was not a dream.

October 15

Yesterday's relentless rain and high winds brought down the last of our colorful leaves. Some now lie on the forest floor, and others blew onto roadways and into gutters. The rain continues today but is a steady, light drizzle, bringing cold and dampness to the mountain. It reminds me of another October afternoon many years ago. No mists were weaving through the pines then. There were traffic lights and horns, tall buildings, a cold, fine rain, and someone was with me. We were in New York City where I eventually came to live.

I was informed of my twin sister's existence and her abortion on my twenty-first birthday. My mother and grandmother sat me down in the studio apartment that mom and I shared in New York City. Granny was visiting.

With solemn faces, they told me what I initially thought to be an impossible tale. I had a twin sister, but she was aborted. A life-threatening blood disease almost killed my mother, yet I survived it all. In a rapid sequence, my mind formed questions. Why did they tell me this? What was to be gained? Was it even true? Did they intend to upset me on this milestone birthday? If so, why? It was incredulous listening to this tale of my almost non-birth. More distressing, though, was the bone-chilling wintertime wrapping itself around my heart. And yet, since childhood I intuitively felt that some part of my being, or soul, was missing, leaving a tiny hollow place in my heart.

In early October 1964, a few months following my revelatory twenty-first birthday, I came face-to-face with the truth of Lily's death during a dreary, rainy afternoon on Thirty-Third Street in New York City.

My father decided to make an impromptu visit to see-the-sites. I thought he might be there on a pretext to see my mother for their mutual anger and disdain towards each other had finally culminated in divorce.

Dad and I wandered to the usual tourist places. After a long morning of walking in damp, bone-wearying weather, we stopped for lunch at a pub on Thirty-Third Street just off Fifth Avenue. We finished our meal and ventured out into the fine mist with the last of the gold and sienna leaves floating down from the City's sidewalk trees. My heart hammered away as adrenalin poured into my system. Every muscle in my body tensed with spasms, silently screaming *now is the time!* This was the moment to ask about my birth and my sister's death, and so I did. "Is it true, dad, that you and mom tried to abort me, and I lost my twin sister?" In mere fractions of seconds, his face and eyes displayed a range of emotions from sorrow to anger, then incredulity, revealing the truth at last. I knew then I had hit marrow. He asked, "How did you learn this?" I told him about my birthday discussion with mom and Granny. He said, "That bitch! This was something you were never supposed to know or needed to know." My dad's eyes brimmed with tears that eventually trickled down his cheeks. In a choked, barely audible voice he uttered, "I am sorry you have learned this. I am so sorry."

He said nothing more. He did nothing more. He just turned and walked slowly down the street in the rain. I stood there stunned and confused, finally accepting the raw truth. I was on an emotional seesaw wanting to forgive him but hate him too. I did not move for what seemed a long time. My hair, soaked with rain, clung to my head and neck while black mascara streaked down my face, though not from tears. My heart cracked within me. I felt a small, quiet, steady cry within for someone to love me, please love me, in that moment of reality. And the baby wail within evolved into tiny tears of blood. Though the tears and blood were not physical, they were real enough in my now-empty, stony heart.

My father and I did not speak for fourteen years after that incident. And in the following decades after the fourteen-year silence, our communications were infrequent and strained. These were fallow periods in which I struggled to overcome shapeless demons that plagued me about my true feelings for him.

I attempted to see beyond the crippling challenges of my birth, a high-strung mother, and my parents' mutual pain and guilt. There were recurring nightmares of my mother walking towards me with a large kitchen knife dripping blood, and eventually my panic and heartbreak at not being wanted in this world invaded my physical and mental well-being. My self-worth was shattered and I was suicidal.

These were the years of multiple marriages, uninhibited anger, and outrage at anyone who displeased me. I sought relief going from therapist to therapist along with one new pill after another to ease the internal war. Suicidal thoughts persisted, more medications were prescribed only to exacerbate my depression. Alcohol was my drug of choice. I drank in a highly controlled manner for several years but eventually spiraled into the depth of addiction. I needed to drink. There was no compromise. I carried a sterling silver flask when I flew on business trips to ensure I had the Stolichnaya vodka I craved. I initially found sobriety and refuge in the rooms of AA on my fiftieth birthday, but there was a significant aspect to this part of my story. Abstinence alone did not replace the hole within me, for it was vast and deep and dark. I was merely not drinking. It would be several more years before I walked from darkness into light.

I remained in New York City for thirty-eight years while these wounds directed the choices in my life. I lived in a beautiful West Village loft for a time until I found this cabin and started life anew. Work with one therapist who remains a caring, loving listener to this day, helped me to move from internal wars to a modicum of calm and balance. Though on shaky ground, I learned to have a little compassion, rather than disdain, toward myself. This self-loathing was clothed in arrogance and projected on to people, places, and things. I felt superior and entitled to belittle and criticize others and the world at large. I hated most people and most things. Very little pleased me. There was no joy in my heart except when I spent money. The awareness I could no longer live with attitudes and offensive behavior that caused harm and pain to others was bitter to face yet a walk I had to walk. However, we are not born to hate. We are taught how and what to hate, and my parents were perfect role models for these teachings.

The unpleasant reality for me was that my father's life force gave me mine, yet my sister was denied her right to live, to have a voice. It took me these many years to discern the integrity of my father's existence, the role he played and did not play, in my life and in the lives of others.

Cleveland, Ohio is where my little-girl-memories were stored in small mental-folders neatly labeled Things That Hurt, When Dad Said Something Nice, The One Time He Played a Game with Me, and When He Burned All My Dolls, Diaries, and Short Stories. These were pale specters that came to reside in my heart and soul during those years of emotional darkness.

Though dad financially supported my childhood creative endeavors, paying for dance and acting classes, costumes, and much more, he understood little about my young aspirations. Performing for live audiences and on television from a very young age, especially as a dancer, consumed my early life. In my father's defense, there was no framework in his experience to understand my childhood uniqueness. We attempted through many years to bond, but these efforts were awkward, filled with anger and pain, shame and guilt—a weighty quartet of emotions.

Dad was not around much when I was a child for he worked two jobs to provide for our family. As a fireman in Cleveland, he was required to work evening shifts several nights a week and drove a Brinks armored truck on his days off. He was a dedicated, hard-working man.

My mother was a homemaker and a clinically depressed woman. According to mom, my very presence caused a chasm between dad and her, lasting their respective lifetimes. She claimed my father insisted upon an abortion for he believed they could not afford to raise another child. *Yes, there was and is another.* Mother was divorced with a six-year-old son, Brad, when dad met her. My brother's presence in my early life was significant.

The truth between my mother and father will never be known. However, my parents believed Lily's abortion was a success. A few months later I alerted them to my presence with a small kick in my mother's womb. They were in shock, and it was too late in that decade to expunge me.

Ten years later my father spat words at me: "I wish you had never been born." I sat in the middle of our yellow and white linoleum kitchen floor sobbing. His words were stinging arrows. I was a child caught in the mutual hatred between my mother and father, a daily, tangible reminder of what they did not want. At the age of ten, though, I believed my father's harsh words were said for me to absorb as absolute.

My mother had fertile ground upon which to build an arsenal of reasons to maintain her intense dislike of my father. He was mean and harsh, stingy, quick-tempered, humorless, unloving, and critical. Sadly too, he was a racist and an anti-Semite.

In high contrast with those behaviors, it was my father who always came to my bedside to soothe my childhood nightmares, colds, and coughs. Dad's fail-safe remedy was to rub my chest with Vicks VapoRub together with a hot drink of lemon, honey, and…Scotch.

When I was eighteen years old living in New York City, I had a serious automobile accident. It was my father, once again, who drove all night from Ohio to keep vigil at my hospital bedside. Mom was there too but left as soon as he arrived. Through the years I've thought about the guilt and shame they must have felt if not on a conscious level, then certainly in their souls.

Life is not simple, nor clear. The markers in the road provide choices tempting us onto questionable highways. Which one to take? Do we march ahead to the stratagems of our own self-centered mind-chatter? The gritty reality is that life in our complex human form is filled with joy as well as sorrow. It is a certainty. Nevertheless, we have a choice, free will, in how we react to peace and happiness, sorrow and pain. These are either adversities and we are victims, or they are our lessons, material for making us stronger, bringing us closer to the intrinsic nature of our existence.

This is not the final chapter of my father's story. There were other factors at work you need to know first. Occam's Razor does not apply here, for nothing in the previous and future sequence of events was simple.

December 1

The winds are at gale force with gusts shaking the windows, creating creaks and unwelcomed groans from the tall pines that have withstood more storms than years I've lived. The snowfall from this nor'easter is already eight inches. It will continue throughout the day.

The wood stove is pumping hard already emitting a cozy fire for my early morning musings. Henry sleeps on the desk while I brew a fresh pot of Assam tea. I am stalled again, but in defense of myself, I needed to put the writing aside to gain perspective, distance too, before I unfolded the next piece of the story.

The nor'easter was forecasted for days, so I spent yesterday in preparation. I bought enough food, water, and other necessities to last two or three days for it may be that long before my private road is plowed. Throughout the day, I brought wood and kindling into the cabin stacking it in several large log holders so I would not run low, nor need to go outside. I set up a litter box for Henry in the event the storm was too fierce even for him to venture outdoors.

Dawn's subdued light appears and what I see from my writing desk through the bay window is a winter extravaganza. Walls of snow continue to descend on every branch and limb, stone wall and fence, bush and tall reed outlining everything in pure crystalline white. Huge flakes and winds swirl into drifts, making unusual designs in odd places creating obstruction to much-needed areas of accessibility. I still see my truck, well, half of it, but for how much longer I do not know. I have an automatic generator should we lose power, so we are safe and secure. Henry and I are more than comfortable. The journal is open to a blank page. My fountain pen rests next to it waiting for me to start again. I am ready.

I've already revealed there were four people directly involved in the events of my sister's death. My mother and father, Lily, and my Granny—my four-foot-eleven-inch tall maternal grandmother.

When a snowstorm arrived in Granny's time, it was like a fairy tale. Her house was old and comfortable and filled with love. I'd gaze out the living room window watching the white, billowy wood smoke pump steadfastly from old cook stoves and large fireplaces. The smoke wafted through the air from known and unknown places with untold stories. Serpentine trolley car tracks glistened on the wet streets. Her living room fireplace crackled with huge logs, while Grandpa Joe sat in his rocker smoking his pipe. Sweet and pungent aromas were everywhere. The scent of snow, cradled in the wombs of steel-gray clouds, stood poised for the right moment to birth sizeable, white flakes that fell outside the warmth and charm of Granny's home.

Not so very different from my little-girl memories, the snow today blusters and swirls burdening the limbs of trees while sketching outlines of ordinary things generally overlooked. An elusive bluebird flies from limb-to-limb with ease and grace. Grave sites and the rumor of haunted mausoleums in our rural cemetery are softly christened in a pure white blanket of snow at the hour when dusk makes its entrance and the flakes come to rest on sacred ground. Through my writing desk window, the snow fashions a serene, ethereal landscape in which no living being ever inhabited. Yes, this is the time, when the snow falls, I remember Granny the most. And, she was the only one who held Lily in her hands.

Granny was born poor and died poor, yet had a heart overflowing with love, a spirit that soared with joy, and a deep, quiet source within from which sprang abundant courage. Granny was five years old when she crossed the Atlantic Ocean from Austria to America in 1899. She was not schooled but taught herself to read, write, and speak fluent English. When I was old enough to understand spoken words, I never detected a hint of accent though I knew Granny spoke Russian, Polish, and German in addition to her mastery of the English language.

In 1950, trolley car tracks created crisscrossed patterns in the streets of the northeast Cleveland, Ohio neighborhood where my grandmother lived. Once I negotiated the snow-covered cobblestone walkway to her house, I stepped on to the wide-planked wooden front porch, stamped the snow from my boots and slipped them off before entering her living room through a dark oak entrance door. I passed through a mahogany arch into the dining room and walked the long, narrow hallway leading to my grandmother's sanctuary, her kitchen.

Few things thrilled me more as a child than the many aromas sent forth from the kitchen where Granny performed the healing of souls through her culinary arts. Six decades later, the mere thought of her homemade Scottish shortbread comprised of those decadent yet straightforward ingredients of creamed butter, sugar, and carefully sifted flour baking in her Franklin wood cookstove, sparks a memory I hold dear. *She offers me her large, well-used wooden spoon — the one that stirred so much in so many bowls and belonged to her mother and her mother before her. I lick the last remnants of sweet dough, a bit of heaven.*

Granny was a force of love, offering the warmth and light I sorely needed in my life as a child and young woman. She had a salty sense of humor, was whimsical, irreverent, and flirtatious. As a Roman Catholic, she prayed three rosaries daily. She added a fourth rosary one summer's day after releasing a particularly nasty, noisy bird through her kitchen window. The bird was a gift that Grandpa Joe brought home for her that past Easter. But not unlike an accordion, she added and subtracted rosaries to her daily prayer routine. This depended on whether she thought she failed or succeeded with the Lord that day, hoping that the Blessed Mother would intercede for her.

While her faith sustained her to a point, she was most serene when preparing and serving a meal. Her Austrian, Polish, and Russian heritages created culinary alchemy for delicacies still not well-known to too many people: Granny's light, fluffy liver dumplings in homemade beef broth, and her unsurpassed pierogi.

For the uninitiated, a pierogi artfully created is a spiritual experience. Granny's pierogis were perfectly round pouches, three inches in diameter, of carefully rolled dough filled with pure ecstasies for one's palate. My favorite filling was Farmer's cheese that she seasoned with salt, pepper, a hint of sugar, thinly chopped onion and a beaten egg to hold the mixture together. She would also fill these round orbs of dough with prunes, or sauerkraut with caraway seed, or a pungent meat mixture.

I sat and watched this artist at her work as she gathered the many and varied ingredients needed to begin the painting of her canvas. The Food consisted of flour, spices, sugar, meats, cheese, prunes, potatoes, cabbage, green peppers, onions, eggs, butter, salt, and pepper. The Tools assembled were a rolling pin, flour sifter, potato masher, meat grinder, one rimmed glass three inches in diameter, waxed paper, rubber bands, cleaned (and ironed) kitchen towels, and mixing bowls. All six bowls were in graduated sizes but did not match. And the essentials were Granny's largest black iron cauldron in which to boil water and her substantial iron skillet, more waxed paper, and The Wooden Spoon.

The last task to complete before the cooking process began was the preparation of the white enameled kitchen table, a perfect square. Granny wiped it spotlessly clean. She then removed her thin gold wedding band and put on a fresh, crisply ironed apron. Finally, she placed the kitchen stool at the table for herself and removed all but one of the six chairs. The concession of the one chair was for me. Granny wanted no encumbrances around the table when she prepared pierogis. I was her honored guest.

For Granny, the making of pierogis was her ministry. To the eight-year-old girl sitting at her table, mesmerized by the unfolding of this grand performance, it was the result that counted most. Granny stored many of the pierogis in her short, square icebox for eating at our holiday dinner. But, she reserved a few to be consumed immediately, and I had my choice. I could eat the perfection of her pierogis as they emerged from the boiling water in the black iron cauldron then covered with chunks of sweet cream butter, salt, and pepper. Or, she would turn to the large iron skillet where she slathered even more butter lowly sautéing the pierogis to a light, golden brown. The result was a transcendent experience. The ingredients of butter, salt, lightly fried dough, and a spicy-yet-sweet cheese and onion filling, were all interdependent, for one single element could no longer exist in this excellent state without the other.

My grandmother cooked for all occasions, and for no reason at all but for the pure pleasure of creating and pleasing others. The latter being a result of her heart's desire and not a conscious goal.

Granny also put on her apron and took to the stove during times of great sorrow. The most vivid for me was when Grandpa Joe succumbed to lung cancer resulting from his many years of work in the coal mines of Ohio. I was thirteen when Grandpa Joe died. After leaving the sterile smells and bleak atmosphere of the hospital, I knew her thoughts were only of her husband, friend, lover, and nemesis at times, as we walked into her now empty home. Granny had to be thinking that Grandpa Joe would walk through the door at any moment. Freshly brewed coffee, as well as his much-loved beer with a raw egg floating in it, would usually be at the ready. Grandpa was a heavy drinker and alcohol addiction prevailed on my mother's side of the family. When we entered the kitchen, she reached into a small closet for her apron and wrapped it around her plump waist. I stood watching not knowing what to say or do. I too felt the intensity of loss and emptiness. I saw Granny withdraw a hand-embroidered cotton handkerchief from her dress pocket to wipe the tears that finally surfaced and trickled down her face. She then turned to me following the long silence and said, "I absolutely must make a pot of chicken soup with homemade noodles."

My memories are continual reminders that the contentment of Granny's open heart, consisting of simple, elegant acts of love and work, was far more essential than any luxury and wealth that she would ever desire, or indeed know.

Granny's riches were imbued in her calloused, square hands, her strong arms that rolled dough for great lengths of time without tiring, and her intuitive sense of touch, taste and innate sensitivity to what was right, or not. This was her art form as well as her medicine, and it could not be captured or repressed. Not even my grandfather's death accomplished that.

Granny was my advocate with my mother and buffered many of the rages and verbal assaults directed towards me. She came to live with us off and on, and I suspect it was due to Grandpa Joe's drinking problem. I saw bruises on her arms from time-to-time. Nevertheless, she brought laughter and love into our lives. And when I visited her home, the joy was even more abundant. Why my mother hated her mother and father so much was never revealed. It is one of those threads in the tapestry that will remain a mystery. After my twenty-first birthday revelation about Lily, Granny never uttered another word. I did not ask her either. Lily's death was between my parents and me. My Granny's love of who I was, not a dancer, or special, or sickly but just a little girl and then a young woman, is etched into my soul. Her unconditional love saved my humanness through the hardest times in my young life. I may not have been fully aware of it as I churned through darkness, but her love never left me. It is stored in my heart. I loved her. I loved her very much.

Granny is with me today as the snow falls and I recall her legacies of great wealth enriching my life. I was working in New York when she died and, sadly, informed three months later. I was prevented from saying goodbye. The animosity between my mother, her brothers, and my own brother was fierce. Their hatred of mom and hers of them was tangible. I inquired about this divisiveness but was told by my mother that I didn't need to know. To this day when I think back upon these matters, I am left with only confusion and speculation. No truth.

Years later, Arthur and I were in the Swiss Alps crossing over into Italy where we came upon a small ruin of a Catholic church in the middle of nowhere. The church sat among wildflowers. There were a few cows grazing with large clunky bells hanging around their necks—apparently the church's only visitors. The church had a partial roof with most of the statues destroyed, but Arthur noticed there were votive offerings with lit candles.

In that ruin of a church resting high in the Alps years after Granny passed, I told her of my deep love for her and thanked her for the many joys she brought into my life. I said a brief prayer, lit one of the candles, and said my farewell.

While Arthur and I hiked down the mountain path, I thought if heaven exists, then Granny and Lily are together now. I would lie if I denied that I haven't wondered about their conversations. What *would* Granny say to Lily who was a small, lifeless baby held in her strong hands? And, *what* would Lily say?

People often ask me how I came to love tea, including the art of brewing it. This too was a legacy from Granny. When I was older, we had dinner in a restaurant with antiques for sale. My eyes kept wandering to an elaborate oriental tea set. The porcelain tea cups were so thin one could see through them. Granny, virtually penniless, purchased it for me. I learned from her to warm the teapot, to fill it with an extra teaspoon of tea for the "happiness" of the pot, to pour the water at the boil, to brew for four to five minutes at the most. She instructed me first to pour milk into the cup and then the tea. Years later, visiting London on many business trips, I could not have learned anything more from watching the British at High Tea than what Granny taught me to do.

Thank you, Granny. Your presence was an overflowing of blessings in my life.

December 15

The view from my windows displays a landscape frozen-in-time. Our temperatures dipped to ten degrees below last night. Snow and ice shine like crystal beads on tree limbs, twigs, and anything it sits upon. We've had one storm after another since the nor'easter. The results are an expertly plowed road, with nine feet of snow pilings around the property. Moreover, it is only December. I've turned on the backup electric heat, and the wood stoves in the living room and bedroom are red hot. Henry stayed with me throughout the night. This was a special treat for I rarely have his heartbeat near me once darkness arrives. Since outdoors is an ice-world today, I won't be walking unless Hank, one of Dave's old friends who continues to help me with chores, brings salt and sand for the road. Much of the recent snowfall arrived in large, soft floating flakes. It is lake-effect snow. The cabin is part of a significant snow-belt pathway. We are high enough that if it rains in the valley, it snows on this mountain.

Anna called to say her pipes were frozen. I said, "Come over if you need water or a shower. Food too. Whatever. Have you seen Peddler?" Anna replied, "He walked to a woman's place in Pennsylvania."

"What? Does she live in a tepee too?" Anna said she didn't know and didn't ask.

With the warmth of the wood fires, the comfort of having an auto-generator, Henry close at hand, nowhere to go with nothing pressing to do, I sit down and look at the blank pages of the journal. It waits for me. It is time to reveal other vital events in this story.

My mother was exotically beautiful, tall and slender with a smooth satin olive complexion that deepened to rich sienna by merely sitting in the summer shade. Her eyes were large and brown and seductive, especially when she laughed and tossed her wavy auburn hair cascading to her shoulders. My father said he married her for her laugh. It was intense and sexy, but only when she wanted it to be.

When she was nineteen years old, she acquired a one-ounce bottle of Shalimar perfume. How or under what circumstances I do not know. What I do know is that she was not in a financial position to buy a one-ounce bottle of perfume, assuredly not Shalimar. Mom completed high school at fifteen, married her first husband at sixteen, divorced at nineteen and during those years gave birth to a son, named Brad who, when I was born, became my half-brother.

During my childhood, she recounted ad nauseam the story of that favorite bottle of perfume, perhaps because she treasured it so and what happened to it destroyed an aspiration, a deep longing within her. It seems that my brother at four years of age walked to her bedroom vanity, reached for the Shalimar, unplugged the stopper, and poured the sweet-smelling essence over the rug, bed, and curtains. This was not a malicious act on Brad's part, but merely the result of a curious, Puckish four-year-old. And to the day of this writing, Brad remains Puckish and irreverent about many things. He made me laugh as a child, something we were in short supply of in our home. He continues to this day to make me smile.

Sadly, our mother in a dark, hidden, twisted part of her mind never forgave him.

This all happened before I arrived in the family. The earliest year of which I have any clear memory is 1947. I was heavily drugged due to childhood epilepsy called Jacksonian seizures, which affected my left arm and leg. It manifested in my staring straight ahead, unaware of anything around me, while needles and pins stung my left arm and leg. I do not recall the seizures as painful. However, I experienced the EEGs involving needles pushed into my scalp and glue used to keep the needles in place, to be more than enough pain. Once I was home, mom pulled the glue out of my hair so she could wash my scalp clean. I remember cruel, stark-faced nuns and nurses leaving me for long periods of time in dark cubicles while a machine recorded brain waves from my scalp stinging with pain.

I recall 1947 for two totally unrelated reasons. One was that the Cleveland Indians hired Larry Doby, the first black man to play in the American League, following Jackie Robinson, who had been signed by the National League for the Brooklyn Dodgers. These facts were presented when I was a bit older, but my mind's recollection summons a night when one of Doby's first games was played. My parents and brother leaned in close to the radio while I lay on the sofa with a high, persistent fever yet to be identified other than flu. Through the befuddlement of medications and a high temperature, I do remember the excited voice of the announcer talking, even yelling at times.

The second reason was devastating to my parents and one I did not yet understand. A few days after that historic game when my fever finally broke, my left arm and leg were paralyzed. I had polio.

The pathway for my future was created through poliomyelitis, and my mother's willingness to embrace her four-year-old daughter's idea. I resisted the accepted forms of physical therapy for this disease. I wanted to study dance instead. My girlfriends were taking ballet and tap, and I wanted to do the same. Dad was not convinced but yielded to my mother's pressure and my stubbornness.

While this was a seemingly impossible feat, somewhere in my four-year-old mind I sensed I could use my own body's movement to overcome the paralysis rather than a physical therapist doing it for me. I started private dance lessons with a steel brace on my left leg and a left arm that barely moved, appearing spastic and clumsy to my teacher I am sure, yet his constant encouragement gave me the strength to continue.

I practiced every day falling repeatedly, creating a bruised, bloody right knee time and again, scraped elbows from the tumbles, and sprained wrists from breaking my falls. Nothing stopped me though from my mission. A year-and-a-half later, my brace broke off during a dance lesson. I could bend my knee and began turning my ankle. The muscles and range-of-motion in my left arm and leg were fully restored within a few months. I was healed from polio to everyone's amazement and the doctor's embarrassment for having condemned me to being disabled for the rest of my life. I loved dancing. I practiced at every opportunity, for I knew that the art of dancing would change my life. As I remember these scenes, had I known what would unfold, I would still do it again. Yes, I would take on polio and do it all over again.

Though my mother supported my efforts, she was not a progressive, courageous, loving parent. She was incapable of any kind of nurturing love during my childhood and young adult years. As for so many, our family was wounded, dysfunctional, and unloving. Pain and suffering exist in our humanness. Sometimes, just sometimes, a little too much is piled on. It was this way with our family.

Two vivid memories of my mother reveal her madness and cruelty. The first of these memories is when she turned her back on me after a kindergarten play because I misspoke one of my lines. Does this sound foolish? I assure you it was not. The other, far more severe, concerned my brother, Brad.

We were in the middle of a massive December snowstorm, the kind that slammed northeast Ohio with great regularity. After a kindergarten performance, in which I played an angel and misspoke one of my lines, was finished, I scanned the audience for a wave or some acknowledgment from her. She glared at me, turned, and left me on the platform stage. Not a word, nor gesture. With a growing awareness that I must have done something wrong, I followed my mother but couldn't maintain her pace, for I was dragging my left leg with the brace on it. Yet, she continued her steadfast march towards home. She never slowed or stopped to check on me. All I saw were her hunched shoulders wrapped in a thick, red woolen coat, almost savage in its blood-red color against the heavy, white, wet snow. When I reached our house, taking my seat at the kitchen table, she said, "You are never, ever to humiliate me again by making a mistake, especially in public. Do you understand me?" Her enraged voice, the sound of a high-pitched warning siren, brought me to tears. I surrendered. In a barely audible whisper, I replied, "Yes mother." I believe my performing arts career began at that moment.

    I disappointed my mother many times through twenty odd years of performing professionally, and each time I encountered another rage accompanied by a cruel critique. I felt like Pip in *Great Expectations* when Miss Havisham and Estella mercilessly belittled him. Yet, Pip survived and so did I. My mother's disappointment with my imperfect performance following the kindergarten play was hotly branded into my soul for many years. While I took psychological blows from mom, my brother suffered far worse.

    I witnessed one occasion in terror, crying out, "Mommy, please don't hurt him anymore, he is bleeding. Why are you doing this?" My cries and pleas were ignored as mother screamed, "You're a stupid, foul boy! You're worthless and will be a bum your whole life. Damn you to hell." These words were accompanied by her beating Brad's head repeatedly against the kitchen wall.

    She then opened the door to our basement and kicked Brad down each step as he bounced off the cement walls with her blows.

Brad's forehead revealed a bloody gash above his left eye and bruises were on his arms and elbows, probably his ribs too. When my mother stopped what seemed an unstoppable rage, Brad ran up the steps, slamming the side door of our house as he made his way out and away from her, an action I witnessed again and again during the years he lived with us.

I huddled on the floor in terror with tears frozen on my face. Brad was thirteen years old, and I was six. The egregious act causing my mother's outrage was that Brad brought home the wrong bread from the local mom-and-pop grocery store where fresh bread was baked daily.

Mom hated the world, and I will never know why. She beat my brother regularly, and I will never understand why. She tried to kill her babies, instead of fighting for us. She did not love her family. She hated her father and despised mine. She belittled her mother, my Granny, unmercifully. And, I will never know why.

These events remain a mystery for there is no one now, sixty years later, who can shed light on her darkness. My dad didn't speak of it, and my brother numbed his pain in alcohol. They locked their respective memories concerning my mother in fortresses deep within themselves. Dad was unable to bear a reopening of these wounds. My dear brother does not and cannot claim our mother as his own even today. (Another death occurred while in the final writing stages of this narrative. Brad too succumbed to lung cancer. We spoke for six months two-to-three times a month. We reviewed our lives, laughed, cried, and healed wounds each of us carried concerning our childhood. Brad was brave in the face of death. I was, and am, so proud of him. He maintained his irreverent sense of humor up through the last phone conversation we had before he died two weeks later.)

While mom was essential, some would say, the primary ingredient in my life story, no one knows the whole tale. That belongs to me. I am the one who was the witness. I am the one who survived.

Through her depressions and rages, she was capable of much creativity. I watched her create beauty in our home on a limited, almost stingy allowance from my father, develop her own innate sense of style in clothes, and surround herself with exquisite use of color and form. She was bold in her imagination and intellectual curiosity. But her talents were feared, ignored, and laughed at by my father, her parents, and everyone else who knew her except for me.

I continued in the performing arts for twenty plus years. I believed then my creativity would have languished without my mother's desire and drive to help me actualize it, and my mother would not have continued to exist without my creativity. I was her lifeboat. I lived to serve her needs. But, she served mine too. I endured my mother's ranting and raging against life, against the world, because my intuition, even as a young child, told me that her creative energy would become mine.

December 24

Anna and I decided to celebrate Christmas Eve decorating a freshly cut pine tree from the property. We baked a veggie lasagna with crisp salad greens, and slathered sweet cream butter on a homemade baguette, courtesy of Anna's baking skills. I made a lemon cream pie. Not traditional, I know, but it's the only dessert I'm capable of producing that has merit in taste and esthetic presence. These were our gifts to one another.

There was such joy in observing Henry's eyes widen once the hundreds of tree lights were lit. Anna brought hand-quilted angels and stars for the low branches in anticipation Henry might want to play. I was excited and curious for I'd never seen him play indoors. He pondered them but opted to sleep under the twinkling tree instead. Maybe he'll play tomorrow.

While taking a short walk after dinner, snow began its graceful descent on to an already crunchy, snow-packed road. We used an old oil lamp to light our path. We were silent, for the most part, but expressed gratitude for our enduring friendship and recounted the blessings in our lives. After Anna left, I sat out on the back deck trying to catch snowflakes on my tongue as they landed on my hair and eyelashes. A haiku, puzzling my head all day, started to untangle itself. I walked back inside to scribble it into the journal, set up the wood stove for the night, packing it with small and large logs, then closed the damper just enough to allow a little air. By morning there will be a thick bed of coals. Henry was in bed. Perhaps he knows it's almost Christmas and that I would love to wake in the morning with his 747-engine purr beside me. I turned off all the lights except for those on the tree. Before falling into what I believed would be an enchanted slumber, I started reciting the first line or two of PSALM 23, "The Lord is my shepherd, I shall not want." A moment before I fell asleep the lines of the haiku coalesced as they drifted through my head. At last. At last! I smelled the sweet scent of fresh pine as I drifted into sleep listening to the silence of snow falling.

snow rests on branches
ushering a quiet peace
sacred time awaits.

2004

*I will instruct you and teach you in the way which you should go.
I will counsel you with My loving eye upon you.*

~ Psalm 32:8

March 18

The winter was long with days of overcast skies and unending lake-effect snow. I stopped writing the story. I was consumed with photography and painting. There were a couple of local exhibits I committed to doing a while back.

After the horses, after Dave, the barn sat fallow. I decided to renovate the top floor, once a hayloft, into a painting and photography studio. Dave may have been prophetic, for he insisted on sliding glass doors at both ends of the twenty-five hundred square foot space, each with small balconies. He said, "You may want to take a break and sip tea. These balconies provide just enough room to sit and breathe. You're high. Keep the camera ready for eagles."

I brought electricity, plumbing, and heat to the top floor for the essentials, including proper lighting for my work, and water for my slop sink, bathroom, and a modest kitchenette. There are skylights too, enabling me to work with natural light most of the time.

I did not take pen to paper this winter, for I lost myself in the visual work and the smells of mineral spirits, oil paints, and beeswax for my encaustic pieces. My wide-screen computer monitor and large photographic printer reside in a space protected from light and reflection. The floor is spattered with paint and wax, and the area is alive when I work in it. To say I am blessed is an understatement. I felt Dave's energy and joy through the weeks of renovation. I was finally doing something I loved and breathing life into something he created.

The process of exhibiting my work again inspired an idea to open a gallery in the village. My worldly-work, consisting of consulting jobs, will help sustain it financially, if necessary. I'd open Thursdays through Sundays. It will reduce my proclivity for reclusiveness. Good? Bad? It's a thought. It would demand I spend more time in my studio, leaving less time for writing.

Tomorrow I depart for a month-long photo shoot. It is difficult for me to leave this sanctuary, Henry, and Shakespeare. Anna will stay here in my absence and care for him while starting spring clean-up on the property.

March 19

I'm driving south on the I-95 corridor in my Ford 150 to do a photo shoot on an Island off the southwest coast of Florida. Once I arrive at Pine Island, the launch point, I can only take a boat to the Island, or as Arthur calls it, paradise. There is no bridge, for the Island does not permit cars. No horns. No fumes. No traffic lights. Just white, clamshell sandy paths and beaches. I'll be there for a month. After driving five or six hours a day, I write these journal pages in the evenings. It relaxes me.

This long drive jogged memories of a time when my life was solely about dancing. I was a dancer. I am a dancer. I dance in whatever I do. Once the brace literally fell off my leg during a dance lesson, I practiced with more attention to the left side of my body to build strength equal to the right. I never stopped practicing. I wanted to be a performance artist, and that is precisely what happened.

I danced every Sunday on local television for Cleveland's own version of *Amateur Hour* when I reached the age of seven. I added to my performance abilities, both acting and voice lessons at the Cleveland Playhouse. When I turned thirteen, I hosted a weekly television show for "younger" up and coming talent. It all flowed to me—almost supernaturally.

It has been fifty plus years since I danced professionally. The act of a flawlessly executed grand jeté, producing a thrilling pirouette, generating articulate, fast staccato tap combinations with the perception of great ease, abandoned my body's abilities long ago. But as a dancer, movement and fluidity, rhythm and grace, were absorbed into the fiber of my being. And yes, the quest for perfection in the arc of my arm, the extension of my leg, the disciplined mornings at the ballet barre, building balance and stamina, followed me throughout these many years. Perfection was my Holy Grail, an expectation insisted upon initially by my mother, but then by me. It was a goal that served me well in my early years. Later, it became a weapon against others including myself. But the spirit of dance is alive within me. Even my photographs and abstract paintings are fluid, and I always search for their music, their unique song. If I do not hear or see something lyrical, I delete it from my body of work.

This extended drive to Pine Island allows me to take short forays off I-95. My motivation is to reach into the past to see if I can recall events, small moments and large ones too, that occurred in the late 1950s. These are experiences few people know about in either my past or present life. I promised a true story, though, and this narrative would be lacking without sharing these seasons in my life. And yes, my mother was involved in it all.

These were the years we traveled the Blue Highways of North America in a white Plymouth packed like the Clampett family in *The Beverly Hillbillies* with all my costumes, our regular wardrobe, pots, pans, toaster, hot plate, cups, bowls, ironing board, iron, soap, and things I can't remember.

From 1958 to 1961, mom and I shared a different quality of time together, venturing beyond the boundaries of what I did, or did not do, on stage. We laughed a lot, often belly laughs, and we cried at the sad and beautiful things we saw on our journeys.

We were awestruck at landscapes and places we'd never seen. The beautiful farmland of the Pennsylvania Dutch Country, Amish carts pulled by horses, the stunning beauty of the Blue Ridge Mountains, and miles and miles of white fencing for horse farms in Kentucky blue grass country. Hearing live jazz played in after-hours clubs. Eating new, great food, as well as awful stuff like a boiled turkey for Thanksgiving dinner in Saskatchewan. Yes, indeed. Canada's Saskatchewan province.

While Saskatchewan was my last memory of Canada, Montreal was my first. We drove to Montreal for a job at a respected nightclub but stayed in a questionable rooming house. These "rooms" were in the Hungarian section of the City.

Mom and I were housed on the top floor, five flights up, in what was once a large closet. It was late-August, and the temperature had been in the high 90s for days. Humid, hot, miserable. We couldn't afford better, and we could not cook for ourselves as was our usual routine to save money. Had we turned on the hot plate, we would've expired. We ate in cheap places when on the road. Howard Johnson's was an elegant treat for us, and they had Early Bird specials. But we were in Québec Province in the city of Montreal. Howard Johnson's did not exist in this French province.

While we were there, we ate in an inexpensive family-run Hungarian restaurant. We could not read the menu written in both French and Hungarian, so we pointed. We ate well, nonetheless. On the second visit, I recognized someone famous. Kevin McCarthy, the star of the movie, *Invasion of the Body Snatchers*.

A confession is in order. My mother and I were science-fiction fans and mom obsessively researched life on other planets and, of course, UFO sightings. Our night drives on lonely roads always led us to search for elusive silver saucers. I've told you this because I was enamored with the movie and Kevin McCarthy. He heard us speaking English, rarely heard in those days in the French province, and asked to join our table. He was teaching a drama course at McGill University for the summer, which was ending soon.

In a few days, I was about to turn sixteen. Kevin arranged for a cake, candles, and gave me my Sweet Sixteen Birthday Kiss. All quite innocent. The memory of that birthday remains fresh and as exciting as it did those many years ago.

The following year we were back in Canada for another job. It was a long drive from Ohio to Québec City. In the pastoral farmlands of Québec, a farmer walked his cart and cows across the narrow, one-lane road. Mom stopped, of course. While waiting for the farmer to cross, one of his cows poked her head into the window on mom's side of the car. Animals liked mom, and she loved them, but she couldn't get the cow's head out of the window. We laughed and giggled almost peeing in our pants. Though we didn't speak French, the farmer somehow understood our laughter and gestures, and finally eased his cow's head out of the window and away from our car with what I believe was an apology for something not his fault.

I fell in love with Québec City, especially the ramparts surrounding Vieux-Québec, the only fortified city walls remaining in the Americas north of Mexico. I never wanted to leave the cobblestone streets, the warm, welcoming owner of a lovely boarding house we stayed in, or the French cuisine, my first, but not my last, croissant, crepes, espresso, and the initial sips of Cognac. Yet, my work ended two weeks later, and it was the first time my agent hadn't found another job for me between Québec City and our Ohio home. We were low on funds, for the Québec City experience cost more than usual. I literally ran to the closest cathedral, which was not hard to find since they resided on every corner or two. I lit a candle to my patron saint, Mother Mary, and prayed a rosary.

Walking back in a light drizzle via a smaller, narrow alley, I saw myself in a discarded cracked mirror wearing a black skirt and charcoal gray blouse. My whole appearance merged into the dark browns and stained brick of old buildings except for the bright red umbrella I held for shelter, the only color marking a presence on the deserted back street. I made a mental note to capture this monochromatic scene with its sole punctuation of color for the future. For what purpose, I did not know. It was a mystery to be discovered someday at another time and place.

As I climbed the stairs and walked into our room, mom hung up the phone and said, "You have a job in Saskatchewan." I hasten to say that I did not claim a miracle based on my rushed pleas for help, and a rosary half-heartedly prayed.

Saskatchewan Province is both prairie and boreal forest. We drove for several days on what appeared to be an endless blacktop, single lane road. The woodland was both beautiful and frightening. Dark, moist, and thick with tall, viridian pines. No gas stations, no diners, no exists. Just one long drive. We must have found gas somewhere, but all I remember is the dense blue-green trees. All fodder for a horror movie, or the short ghost story I wrote while we drove the many miles.

Once arrived, we observed a sprawling farmhouse-style structure sitting in low swampland. I recall navigating the muddy roads and mushy grass walkways. I immediately met with the band and rehearsed while mom got our room together. This is where we had boiled turkey for Thanksgiving and lived with a family of mice in our room for two weeks. It was welcoming to hear English spoken as the band was from Ontario and, the audience was predominantly Anglos.

However, due to the boiled food, bleak landscape, and even bleaker supper club with mice as welcomed guests, we could not wait to leave. I developed a big crush on the tall, fair-haired bandleader who was also the drummer. I got over it.

On another long drive from Ohio to Tyler, Texas we journeyed along the roads of Kentucky's horse farms, winding roadways through small mountains, prairieland, and bits of Tennessee Appalachia mountain towns that were unwelcoming and suspicious of Yankee accents. Mom's dress shoes were stolen somewhere outside of Amarillo, Texas because we forgot to lock the car when we stopped to eat. Miraculously nothing else was taken. Perhaps because every corner and inch of the car was stuffed, it appeared an overwhelming task to take anything more. For one so young, I was somewhat compassionate, if not downright philosophical, saying, "They must have needed your shoes, mom. So be it." Mom did not share my philosophical bent and was, well, thoroughly pissed. I prayed she wouldn't go into a rage.

Our car windows buckled in the heat of summer in Clearwater Beach, Florida. We left them closed when we should have done the opposite. The car battery died in a sub-zero Illinois winter somewhere in Decatur. We were invited to a 3 A.M. duck-hunting breakfast served either in Illinois or Alabama, consisting of more gravy, biscuits, a variety of meats, and desserts than we imagined possible. We did not join the hunt, nor were we invited.

In the years to come, mom and I frequently talked about two driving incidents. One was a horror. The other event, though funny at the time, still occurs and is not the topic for a joke. Okay, maybe it is.

The horror was the pack of wolves we hit on an empty highway at 2 A.M. driving all night to make rehearsal time for my booking in Chicago. There were five wolves. They came out of a black night, no moon, no stars, racing across the highway. We didn't see or hear them until they appeared in our headlights. We smashed through a couple, killing them leaving crushed bodies and body parts on the road. Two others were wounded and howled as they limped off to the other side into the woods. Mom and I never forgot the sight and sound of it all. Bodies hitting our car bumper and grill, howls of pain, and tires rolling over lumps. We found an all-night diner and stopped to assess our vehicle and calm our nerves. The car was bloodied, and the tires were covered in bits of wolf. Mom didn't drink in those days, but this state served liquor, and she ordered a double scotch swallowing it in one long gulp. I had coffee and warm homemade apple pie with ice cream.

The second event occurred on another all-night drive when mom and I spelled one another so we each could each catch some sleep. Fortunately, it was an empty double lane highway, and I was driving about 55 mph when I came to an abrupt stop. Mom woke startled and asked, "Where are we? Is something wrong?" I said, "Mom look! There's a parade of four pink elephants on the highway. Can't you see them? They're crossing the road!" My night-driving for extended lengths of time ended on the spot in the middle of nowhere. I still have the problem, though there are glasses now that help. A bit. I remain careful to this day not to commit to a long-distance drive at night.

I have a lengthy drive tomorrow, and I'm finally tired. You must wonder at this point about a sixteen-year-old girl in nightclubs, possibly in uncertain environments?

Tomorrow. I'll tell you tomorrow.

March 20

My drive through the Carolinas today was long. Whatever product is used to build the roadways in this state shimmers like diamonds in the bright noonday sun. A counterpoint to the glittering highways are the torn tire treads on the shoulders. Miles and miles of shredded rubber. *Why are they left there?* The things we ponder when driving alone for long distances. I hope to make it through Georgia to the Florida border tomorrow. I am eager to reach the Island. I have another two days. The weather is warmer than Virginia, and the warmth is welcome. I am shedding layers and loving it.

The Hampton Inns in which I chose to stay for this journey have Wi-Fi, television (although I rarely watch it), and comfortable beds. And, I have my tea. I packed my electric tea kettle, enough loose tea for my road journey, and a pint of cream I buy fresh each day. And, it's time to continue the story.

The road travels with mom to dance professionally began the summer following my high school sophomore year. I knew what I wanted to do, and that was to dance and sing as a professional performance artist. I made plans in my basement, which dad had converted into a dance studio with a mirror, ballet barre, and flooring.

Though dad was opposed to my desire to perform in nightclub venues, he didn't stand a chance given my abilities to persuade with both logic and pathos. So, he helped falsify my birth certificate. Dad was a captain in the fire department and respected among the powers-that-be. He produced a birth certificate stating I was eighteen, thus protecting any nightclub owner from liability, and ensuring I was indeed a legitimate performer to be hired. I was approached by a decent, competent agent, Vince Schakowsky, due to my already active performance life. I was a card-carrying member of AFTRA (television), Equity (theater), and AGVA (nightclubs). Lots of dues, but I was legally covered to work in all these venues and, in time, would need each one.

My vision was to be an opening-act for the headliner of the show. The task of an opening-act was to warm-up the audience for the star they really came to see. I needed to create twenty minutes of performance time, an bona fide night club act.

I outlined the key elements. The first routine would be a bright, bouncy rhythmed song and dance. Following that, so I could catch my breath, would be a slower routine with modern dance movement. The finale would consist of a knock-out, fast-paced tap routine with drumsticks and staccato taps talking to one another. I lifted this directly from one of Ann Miller's dance numbers in a Fred Astaire movie.

I used vinyl albums for music that fit my choreography, but I needed new music, thoroughly scored for a thirty-two-piece orchestra. Why for a full band? I wasn't sure. However, my primary dance instructor and mentor, David Morgenstern, said I would need it. And, he was right.

I realize how bizarre this may appear to those who led normal teenage lives. But, everything fell into place. David suggested a musician for me to work with for scoring the music. His name was Christopher Lane, a member of the Cleveland Symphony Orchestra, no less. Though I was firm in my mind's vision of each routine, Chris made a valuable suggestion for the second, slower dance routine to use the melody from the movie soundtrack of *Picnic,* overlaid with an older tune, *Moonglow*. It was poetic. And I saw the dance routine clearly: A single spotlight, an ice-blue satin costume shimmering with beads and sequins, and a billowy silk and chiffon skirt floating as I turned and kicked so very high. I thought the audiences would love it, and when actual performance time arrived, they did. Thank you, Chris!

I chose Benny Goodman's, *Sing, Sing, Sing* for my final dance number. This required a lot of scoring and editing for Chris. Goodman's original recorded performance was fifteen minutes, maybe twenty, in length. Chris skillfully pulled the essence of Goodman's music into five minutes creating a rousing closing dance routine. Together, we developed a first-rate opening act, and it served me well.

While mom and I drove the Blue Highways, and I danced and sang in dubious-to-elegant nightclub venues, my mind schemed and planned through that first summer on the road. I did not want to return to school. After some research, I developed a strategy to leave high school yet still complete my diploma via correspondence school. Now that I think of it, I was ahead of my time, only I had no computer. What I had was a portable Smith-Corona typewriter. Dad fought the school issue as I knew he would. My teachers agreed to review my work together with the correspondence school. That satisfied him. And, I was free to live my dream to perform.

Most of my schoolwork was done in various dressing rooms between two nightly shows, as well as writing nighttime stories in daytime hours. There was a richness to the people and their personal experiences. Each nightclub had its known and unknown story. The aged, slightly hunched over waiters saw the best and the worst of people and events telling their tales as part of their personal histories. And, of course, the musicians had their stories filled with excitement, drama, and the sorrows that alcoholism and heroin addictions brought into their lives. Always carrying a notebook, I wrote every day. I loved it.

After moving to New York City, dad never asked me when he sold our home if I wanted any of my childhood dolls and diaries. Moreover, he did not ask about the stories I compiled in many notebooks packaged in a box labeled *My Adventures With Mom*. He burned everything. No. The truth is they were annihilated in a mean, violent act. His was an act of cruelty against my mother, not me. All I have left of those writings are headlines. The details are incomplete or wholly forgotten.

I cannot provide the rich details about stepping on to an auditorium stage on Christmas Day at Michigan State Prison with the second-generation Glenn Miller Orchestra. Ray McKinley, a notable drummer, was now leading the iconic band. Hundreds of prisoners shouted when I walked on stage for I was young, sweet-faced, and wore a pretty costume. They never stopped shouting so much so that I could barely hear my music. When I snapped off my long skirt to reveal a short, emerald-green satin body costume for the *Sing, Sing, Sing* finale, the prisoners yelled, "legs!" Indeed, they saw legs. But then the unexpected. Ray handed the baton to someone else and went to the drums and did what he dubbed the "drum and tap dialogue" with me. The men became silent and listened to Ray's skilled drumming and my fast, clicking taps, each speaking to the other. This was only a fragment of the whole experience.

I cannot tell you about the names, or stories, of the prisoners I wrote to for years afterward, and when it all stopped. The reasons why our mutual correspondence of their lives in prison and mine as a performer ended are also forgotten.

There is little to share with you about the various women, tawdry-to-elegant, with whom I shared dressing rooms, teaching me how to enhance my green eyes with a black wax beading on my eyelashes, or how the local drummer from Woody Herman's orchestra in Decatur, Illinois professed great love for me and was dying, or so he said. I can't tell you about the circumstances around why mom and I were called 'Yankee Hemorrhoids' in Biloxi, Mississippi, and, therefore, I received no applause at all. And what of the older vaudevillian comedienne who told me to ignore it, take the money, and move on? Sarah Yates was her name. Her personal story is a blank.

Somewhere in Texas, I performed in an outdoor stadium with the great Tommy Dorsey Orchestra. My mentor-dance instructor was right. I needed scoring for a full orchestra. But who I met? The star headlining the show? The color of the costume I wore? The memory is faded like a canvas exposed for too many years to the harmful elements of bright sun, dampness and mildew, leaving only an echo of what it once was.

I can no longer retrieve the underlying substance of these stories for they are ash. *Dad, why did you do it? Don't you know that your actions did not hurt mom? These stories were my creative world, a real world with unusual people in an era never to return. It injured me, dad, for mom didn't care.*

March 21

I drove through Georgia today, welcoming the warm sun streaming through heavily budded trees. Spring was about to give birth to the landscape. I didn't know at first what it was about the peanut farmer's hand-painted road sign nailed to a two-by-four, but the instinct to check it out was powerful. The sign read, BOILED PEANUTS-NEXT EXIT.

Then, I remembered.

It began here. Forty-five years ago. Georgia. Red Dirt. Black faces and an old black man wiping his brow with a blue and white bandana. The beginning I refer to is my coming of age. A harsh realization that there are inequities concerning our humanness, our human family. What I witnessed then remains today a parasitic heartless, biased, and brutal reality. It is insidiously subtle yet also blatantly vicious. It takes many different forms in our world today. Aversion, indifference, and disregard yoked with the lack of compassion and kindness for our brothers and sisters, for anyone who does not think as we do, virtually dwarfs and cloaks any good being done.

As I stepped out of my car and walked to the Boiled Peanuts stand, my vision, like pressing the shutter release of my camera, focused in on the exact place and time—Georgia 1959.

Mom and I were driving to Clearwater Beach, Florida for a booking in what was considered an elegant dinner club. We drove through South Carolina most of the day and were finally in Georgia. The memory unlocked by the sight of the peanut farmer's stand was from our experience in the Peach State on a hundred-degree day in the shade.

Whatever the road we were on, it was a single lane without shoulders. I saw shack after shack of barefooted black people. They were called Negroes in the 1950s. From my white Plymouth's passenger window, I looked at tired, worn faces watching the cars go by as they sat on broken steps of narrow, wooden porches. I remember the earth red with clay. I had never seen red dirt. It fascinated me. And, the faces staring at us haunted me.

We were almost out of gas at one point, so we pulled into the only station we saw in a section of a nameless small town where black people lived. We were from the north and our neighborhoods were mixed races and religions. We saw no reason not to stop. When we got out of our sweltering car for there was no air conditioning at that time, we saw a small group of black men, a few dogs and cats, some chickens, and small, skinny children running about in rag-tag clothes. There were no women. The men and children stopped what they were doing regarding us with suspicion. The station had one gas pump. Everything else? Just red dirt. Nothing was paved.

An old black man with thick white hair stepped out from the group of three or four men and with gnarled hands wiped his brow with a large, square blue and white bandana. He looked at my mother and asked, "How y'all doin' ma'am? Would ya and the miss have some pop?" He pointed to a three-foot-high red and white Coca-Cola chest that held glass bottles stacked randomly in hand-chopped ice. With a gentlemanly gesture of his left hand still holding the bandana, he indicated that we should each take a bottle and we did. The old man motioned with his head for us to sit on a weathered bench under a massive tree throwing lots of shade while he filled our gas tank. When mom paid him for the gas, she asked, "How much for the pop?" He replied, "Nothin' ma'am, 'cause it too hot a day to charge y'all for a cool drink." We thanked him and drove back on to the road, leaving a group of people still staring as if we had emerged from a dream.

I could not grasp how these people survived. I had no idea that anyone in our country would be bound to live as they did, and there remain regions in our great nation, where some still do. Decades later I see their faces, the shacks, the poverty as clearly as I did in 1959. Yes, this is where it began. This was the place and time my moral sense awakened.

Today, I stood alone at the peanut farmer's stand holding my camera. He said nothing while I revisited this memory. I asked, "May I take some pictures of your stand?" Not unlike the old black man, he nodded yes, and went about his business while I took pictures of the stand at varying angles. Out of reciprocity for freely taking pictures, I purchased a small bag of fresh, fleshy pecans. And, with some hesitation even after a brief, but informative, discussion on how boiled peanuts are made (lots of salt, a variety of spices, cooked with their shells on in a cauldron of boiling water), I also bought a cup of salty boiled peanuts. Once you've gently cracked the shell with your teeth, the nut has the consistency of a cooked bean. They are quite tasty. I drove away eating pecans and a boiled peanut or two.

This decades-old memory of a wizened black man's generosity in treating mom and me to two cold drinks on a steaming hot day in Georgia still glows in my heart. There was an inherent nobility and kindness in the man. One does not, should not, forget these encounters. They are rare.

Tomorrow the Island.

April 30

I have resided on the Island for one month, a period that moved at an otherworldly, peaceful pace. It is indeed paradise here.

The Island's technical name is North Captiva, because it is above a larger populated island, Captiva. Most locals call it Upper Captiva. When Arthur and I visited the Island for the first time, the atmosphere was not unlike Hemingway's Key West. It was somewhat wild in its landscape with few amenities. We brought in our food and supplies by boat, and this requirement continues today.

I'm staying gratis at Arthur's townhome, not on the Gulf side, but on the Harborside with a view he loves for good reason. The sunrises are painterly, offering a palette of colors that would be the envy of any artist, beginning in deep cobalt blue to rich, dark lavender, then to turquoise of various shades, and finally, pink to azure. The pure white gulls, swooping, and diving, provide an ethereal contrast to the blue-green water and sky. Each sunrise is unique as are the sunsets on the Gulf side, just a five-minute walk from the harbor. To be on our East Coast and see the sun rise over one body of water and set over another is unrivaled for nature lovers. *Yes, the sunrises and sunsets shout for joy!* For my camera and me? Rapture.

I walked forty-six miles during this month taking photographs of flora, fauna, porpoise swimming, the bird sanctuary, which comprises three-quarters of the Island, people, dogs, old sea turtles, weathered beaten gates, abandoned beach shacks, and a circa 1917 tractor, the one that created the first sandy pathways on the Island. I believe this may be one of my better images.

I walked each morning on the white clam-shell beach, watching the dolphins swim along, always with camera in hand. After 4 p.m., I'd take another walk through the interior pathways, discovering new homes, renovated shacks, more flowers, bewildering vegetation, and on one occasion an osprey in full flight. I captured it without camera blur. I was thrilled.

Arthur's townhome is a typical Floridian beach home with light colors, skylights, bright kitchen, salmon-pink bathrooms, and a guest room overlooking the pristine marina and staggering sunrises. On the main floor, there's a screened porch facing the harbor.

Every morning at 4:30 a.m., I sat on the porch with the first pot of freshly brewed Assam tea. I filled a pot-bellied turquoise glazed mug wrapping my hands around this comfortable vessel. Tropical birdsong and soft waves lapped against the shoreline. At 5:45 a.m., I strolled a short one-hundred feet to a silver-gray teak bench at the marina, observing early signs of life stirring dominated by the first boat of the day arriving with Island supplies for restaurants as well as people.

I took more than eleven hundred photos, uploaded them to my laptop, and chose a few to share with a small email group I established before I left. Anna and Arthur were the most important. Since I was driving alone, I wanted them to know where I was while on the road. Once here, I also wanted to share the experiences and visual portfolio of paradise.

My exploration of this quiet, small Island is at an end. The luggage and camera equipment stand at the dock for the 9 a.m. boat to take me to the mainland. My eyes glisten with tears as I walk to where the boat captain stands. Fear and sadness return telling me that this paradise too will pass away from my life. Two doves sitting together on a high branch pulled me out of this gloom. Using the one camera I kept out of my luggage, I capture their divine perfection.

As the boat leaves the dock making its way to the mainland, I watch the Island fade finding the experience bitter-sweet. Though I feel sorrow at leaving, I am also filled with gratitude for the experience of living in a tropical paradise for a moment in time.

May 3

When I began my journey from upstate New York to Florida, I drove for the first two days through pouring rain and dense fog in a monochromatic landscape of gray and brown. For the past two days on my drive home, it has been sunny and seventy degrees with light spring breezes carrying only a hint of winter-past on its breath. Driving through Georgia and the Carolinas, I find delight in the palette of bright, young green leaves on trees side-by-side with the dark viridian evergreens.

I woke before dawn, had my cup of Assam tea, and now walk outside pushing the motel's luggage trolley towards my truck. While I lift suitcases and camera bags off the cart into my truck, a middle-aged woman in a motorized chair appears out of nowhere.

My eyes are on the motel lobby, and I know she didn't emerge from there. She cuddles a small white poodle in her lap as we bid one another good morning. Her dog jumps from the beige blanket in her lap onto the grass and takes care of business. Then the little poodle leaps back into her lap settling in for a pat on the head and a hug. She drives her chair towards an area of the parking lot where there is an unhindered view of the rising sun.

I feel sad, maybe pity. No, it's neither of those. I feel guilty, for I survived. After all, I was in a wheelchair and knew the confinement and dependency imposed on me. Yet, here I am bending, lifting, able to move and stretch my legs and arms while this woman cannot. Had I not learned to dance, this could have been me. I was soon to learn though that my feelings towards her were misplaced. I turn and find her watching me. She says, "Hard work for so early in the morning. Are you traveling alone?" I reply, "Yes, I am." She looks at me with penetrating, warm brown eyes saying, "Well dear, may the angels watch over you and bring you safety and comfort today." I am surprised at what feels like an invocation, a blessing, from someone I don't know. There is a genuine sweetness to her being, yet for a reason not wholly apparent to me, I hold back asking if I might take a picture of her and her dog. Tears fill my eyes when I think of her gracious blessing, for I presumed in my arrogance, to be the healthy, whole person.

I proceed with the seven-hour drive ahead of me, highway only this time, yet once again through the beautiful Blue Ridge Mountains. However, while admiring the views, I narrowly escaped being the centerpiece of a potential ten-car pile-up. Though the highway is a double-lane, there are hairpin turns and many large trucks passing one another. One of these monster vehicles, while pulling out of his right lane, does not see a small car moving on his left. Once the truck's driver hears the car's horn, he slammed on his brakes causing all the cars behind him to swerve and brake. The car in front of me maneuvered to his left allowing me to brake and slide forward. The car behind me, as well as one in the right lane next to me, came within inches of colliding with my truck. Thankfully, no one was hurt, but we were all shaken.

However, the trials of the day did not end there. As I check into my motel room somewhere in Maryland, I notice a very acrid outdoor odor and tell this to the young woman at the front desk, wearing a white flower in her dark brown hair. She said in a sweet, soft southern drawl, "Oh, the farmers were sprayin' chemicals today. That must be what you smell 'cause the winds are blowin' the fumes in our direction." Why I calmly accept this without concern or comment, I do not know except for my extreme hunger. I ask, "Where can I eat dinner?" I was told that the Corner Diner was the only place within many miles.

I love diners. After living in New York City for thirty-eight years, one does not exist without a good local diner. This one was within walking distance of the motel, so I start out for dinner. As I enter the Corner Diner, I know from the loud music, dirty floor, and smell of grease that I am in trouble. I order a grilled chicken salad, which consists of fried chicken, iceberg lettuce, a plastic pouch of Russian dressing sitting on the edge of the plate, and two packets of saltines tossed onto a sticky table.

I do not complain or panic. This is the best they offered. There is a microwave oven in my accommodations, so I have a plan. I fortuitously brought packets of organic instant oatmeal, a small bowl, and a spoon. However, upon my return to the motel, I could not stand the smell in my room. It was different from the fumes outdoors and persistent. With eyes tearing and heart palpitations, I realize I'm experiencing a powerful physical reaction to whatever is causing the noxious odor inside the room. I ask the young woman with the white flower in her hair if I could see the manager who, when she walked into my room, immediately informs me that the smell is the glue used for the newly installed wallpaper and not the chemicals sprayed on the farm crops earlier in the day. I am relocated into a room with old wallpaper and, thankfully, no odor. My new-old room faces the highway and noisy trucks. I refuse to let my spirits be dampened. I am almost home. I eat my handy oatmeal with cream poured into it, watch a disaster movie on the Si-Fi channel in which Chicago was obliterated by an improbable convergence of storms over Lake Michigan.

Putting my earplugs in before sleep enveloped me, I thought about the day starting with the blessing from the angel-at-sunrise. I avoided a major car accident. Apparently, I had not supped well but escaped potential food poisoning and cleared my lungs of toxic fumes. I thought it appropriate to offer thanks to God for I learned today how humility, thinking less of one's self and more of others, is too often a hard lesson for me. I retreated from an opportunity to photograph an angel who most assuredly blessed me. Truthfully, I had an aversion to her disability, and I feel ashamed. Surely the events of this day proved that I needed her blessing. I feel clumsy as I kneel, for it has been many years since I have done so. I thank God for the variety of experiences, from harrowing to beautiful, offering gratitude that I was alive. I add an amendment to my prayer for the angel-at-sunrise who worked overtime today. Or, was it God who managed the miracles? Yes, it had to be God, for the angels obey Him. They do his bidding, or so I've read in the Bible.

Tomorrow I arrive home. The cabin and Henry and Shakespeare.

May 5

Sitting at my desk, I observe what spring has brought to the mountain. Daffodils, crocus, and new green sprouts of things soon to give birth again. A steaming mug of tea sits next to my laptop. I abandoned the handwritten journal notes while traveling, for I was forced to use my computer for convenience. I was uncomfortable at first yielding to this new ease of writing, but I came to like the rhythm with which I could edit. Dangerous for me for I could spend days, and did, editing one page. Henry, my Henry, sleeps next to the computer, while daylight gently climbs over the mountain. Many crows arrive with their harsh cawing, a distinct contrast from the tropical birds on the Island whose songs were softer, lazier, lulling one into dreamland, into paradise. For a few moments, I meditate on mist rising and meandering through the trees and rocks and foliage of the mountaintop forest. And now Shakespeare arrives to sit on his favorite tree limb! Perfect.

I have months of work ahead with the Island photographs. Uploading over eleven hundred to my large screen iMac, curating for Photoshop refinements, then finally separating the wheat from the chaff. Only then do they go to my printers in Kennebunk, Maine. This seems daunting to me now, for I just want to be with Henry, see Anna and Peddler, and walk with my snake stick. I need to spend these summer months, though, doing the hard work on the images while continuing to write the story. I've inserted a consulting project into my timeline as well. There is another month-long photo shoot near Stonington, Maine and Bar Harbor in the early fall. For the first time, I feel pressured by the work I love doing. *Breathe Lee Anne. Breathe.* The best therapy in this moment of rising panic is to arrange dinner with Anna and Peddler. I must see them and share my new work. We'll talk about our mountain, and as they tell their stories, I will sit, listen, and absorb it all. I reach both, and plans for grilled steaks, salad, baked potatoes, and a peach pie via Anna for dessert are in place.

May 6

You may think I've run aground with the narrative, but only with the best intentions. The story does not end with the death of my sister. Nor does it end with mom and me in our Plymouth driving along the Blue Highways, listening to authentic Country Western music of the day with the likes of Johnny Cash, George Jones, Merle Haggard, and Patsy Cline.

Oh, the story ends, but not just yet. You see, there was smooth sailing as well as rocky shores ahead.

I've referenced living in New York City. How and why did it come about? When I was eighteen, mom and I took a Greyhound bus to New York City in April, 1962. I wanted to move there to perform and study rather than go to college. This was another major negotiation with my parents, especially dad.

Mom and I roomed in an apartment hotel filled with roaches at Seventy-Second Street and Broadway, then labeled "needle park" as the top location for drug dealers and users. The pigeons were a noisy and messy presence on our windowsills until we got used to them. Within two weeks of arrival in the City, I started my first job dancing as an opening act at a famous nightclub called the Copacabana. It was a nightspot where well-known singers and comedians headlined. Tony Bennett, Steve Lawrence and Edie Gormé, Paul Anka, Sammy Davis, Jr., Jimmy Durante, and more.

There was an advertisement for Copa Girls in *Variety*, a trade newspaper for theater, music, and nightclubs. Mom and I went to the audition not knowing what a Copa Girl was, but it became evident that these five-foot-nine tall beauties, each with long legs and big breasts, were the definition of a Copa Girl. They were beautiful, not only their breasts but the women too. I was five-foot-four, flat chested, weighing a hundred and ten pounds. I looked absurd standing among them as we began walking around to music played with piano and drums. The director of the show, Doug Gowdy, asked me to step aside, but he did not ask me to leave. He then pointed to several tall girls, thanked them and told them they could go.

He glanced at my mother, sitting in the shadows and asked me who she was. I told him that she'd been traveling with me for a few years, what I did, who I worked with and where. Doug asked if I had any music with me. I walked into the shadows where mom sat, and she handed my music to me as I then handed it over to what became a band of more than a piano player and drummer. *Where did these musicians come from?* I sang and danced the opening number of my nightclub act. Doug asked for a single dance routine. It was *Sing, Sing, Sing*. The drummer, for a first-time without rehearsal, delivered admirably on the tap-drum-dialogue. These musicians knew their craft. I was awarded the job as a featured opening act in a world-famous nightclub in New York City. I was also fingerprinted, which was the law in those days. It had to do with Frank Sinatra and something he did at one point in his career. However, the law was abandoned not too many years later.

The club was owned by the Mafia, but it was of no concern to me. In fact, one of the bouncers walked me to the bus stop every night around midnight and waited with me on the corner of Fifth Avenue and Sixty-First Street until my bus arrived.

There I was within weeks of arrival in New York, rehearsing for a new show to open in ten more days. Once we opened, I was approached by a talent agent. I had been warned to be careful of men with dubious promises and intentions. However, this man told me that Jackie Gleason, a well-established television star, was going back on CBS to do a new musical variety show. He thought I should audition to be one of the June Taylor Dancers, also a household name at that time. I was so thrilled and couldn't wait to tell mom who was, not surprisingly, immediately negative. She reminded me I had never danced in a chorus line, that I was always a stand-alone, featured act. I performed professionally from the age of seven at that point, so I understood her point-of-view. However, these were the June Taylor Dancers on national television! Disregarding her argument, I went to the audition. I had never attended an "open" audition, and a journey of journeys for a nineteen-year-old girl from Cleveland, Ohio began.

Only sixteen dancers were chosen when it was over. Though there were seven hundred and fifty who appeared for the grueling three-day audition, hundreds were eliminated through tests of stamina and equal skills in tap, ballet, and jazz. We were expected to learn complex dance combinations quickly and accurately. This rigor and pressure for six or more hours each day were stoically endured for if anyone showed signs of fatigue, we soon learned the dancer would not make the next round of tests.

Our ability to kick high for exhausting lengths of time was only one of the challenges we faced to surface "the strongest, most versatile, and best-of-the-best dancers" for the demanding choreographer, June Taylor.

It was the final hour of our audition. A large, round electric wall clock with thick black Roman numerals on a white face hung next to an old stained standpipe. It showed the time at four o'clock. Twenty-one dancers out of the seven hundred and fifty that arrived three days ago stood to wait. It was a humid August afternoon, and we were in the mud-brown basement-cum-audition room of the Henry Hudson Hotel on West 57th Street in New York City circa 1962.

We were informed that Jackie Gleason was on his way from his penthouse suite to help in the selection of sixteen female dancers. Along with being physically and emotionally weary, our leotards were saturated with sweat, our hair was wet and clinging to our heads and necks, and little of our face makeup remained due to the previous five hours of constant perspiration.

I heard him before I saw him. Jackie was talking to his colleagues as he emerged from the elevator bank. When he strolled through the double glass doors opening into the basement, I was struck immediately by his gracefulness. Despite his size, he moved so easily, gliding rather than merely walking. His curly raven-black hair, slightly tinged with silver at his temples, set off light-blue eyes that reflected a spirit filled with both *joie de vivre* and an indefinable sadness. He wore a gray suit with a crisply starched white shirt. His necktie was casually loosened. In his jacket's lapel, he wore a boutonnière, an ever-present fresh carnation. Jackie held a cigar in his left hand as he carried a china teacup and saucer. He smiled at us and said something, but with my heart beating loudly in my ears, I couldn't hear him. I knew that within minutes five dancers would be dismissed.

Jackie and the producer of the show joined June at a long makeshift conference table. My gaze was fixed on June's very slender, five-foot-seven body when she stood up from the table and bent her head of shortly bobbed blond curls towards Jackie as she conferred with him over her notes, periodically casting her pale, piercing blue eyes in our direction. She began shuffling some of us around in the line and asked, "April would you please move down by two to the stage-left end of the line? Lee Anne, please stand on April's right. Jamie move to the stage-right end of the line? Thank you." They all looked at us, and June said, "Now, go back to your original positions." Then silence.

June held her many pages of notes contained on a yellow legal pad of paper, asking each of us to call out our names. As we did, she made further notations. Jackie continued smoking his cigar and sipped from his teacup while looking intently at each of us as we announced our names. When it was finally my turn, I thought my voice sounded so small and weak, that it was void of any life signs. Certainly, I had diminished all merit I might have gained over the course of the three-day audition in that brief singular moment. With thoughtful deliberation, June called out the name of a dancer and asked her to step forward. I grew cold and shaky from raw nerves. As she called out three more names, I was sure the dancers now being assembled were those that had been chosen for the show. When she called out the fifth name, there was a suspended moment of silence. Everyone's breathing seemed to stop. June's eyes focused steadily on the group of five. She walked up to each girl, shook her hand, and in her husky-cigarette voice, with only a slight suggestion of acknowledgement and respect said, "Thank you, Jamie, Sandy, Laurel, Cindy, and Meg. You are dismissed."

Sixteen of us remained with rampant emotions from happiness to relief that it was over. However, there was mounting anxiety about the real work ahead. It soon became apparent, though, that we were not yet finished. June asked us to perform once again for Jackie and to do the dance combination we had learned earlier, which involved a protracted series of high kicks. We moved into what would become our permanent positions in the line and June gave the piano player a fast five, six, seven, eight. We pulled ourselves out of weariness into peak performance and kicked high for an extended period until the music stopped.

Jackie applauded, while we inhaled deeply to regain some semblance of normal breathing from what felt like hot, bursting lungs. When I recaptured my equilibrium and looked up again, I saw June. Her eyes reflected her mental assessment of what we had done right, what needed improvement, and who among us required more skill. I shifted my focus and looked directly at Jackie. His blue eyes beamed approval and with a last inhale of his cigar and a wave of his right hand said, "It's going to be a hell of a ride girls, a hell of a ride. How sweet it is."

We were now officially The June Taylor Dancers and opened *Jackie Gleason's American Scene Magazine Show* from New York City on CBS at 8 P.M. every Saturday night from 1962 to 1964. The sixteen dancers ranged in age from nineteen to twenty-six and in height from five-foot-two to five-foot-seven. I was one of the nineteen-year-olds chosen and three other dancers from Ohio were selected as well. There were two sisters from Akron, one a petite blond named Joan, though affectionately called Buttons, the other a sweet-faced brunette with the sensible name of Donna, and April from Dayton who was five-foot-two with uncommonly long legs for someone her height. Her strawberry blond hair framed a small, Episcopalian nose and large, round blue eyes, all of which conspired to herald her Irish heritage. Due to our similar height on camera and the fact that we complimented each other in that she was blond, and I was brunette, we were cast to flank the stage-left side of the chorus line, April at the very end and me next to her. This line-up did not last, but an enduring friendship flourished between us spanning more than fifty-six years. I continue to talk and write to Buttons, Donna, Phyllis, Jari, Mercedes, and Barbara. I've been unable to find the others. Nevertheless, these were my sisters in this brief season-of-life.

Our first official workday began with rehearsal. June walked with strength and purpose into the rehearsal hall to start our work together. She wore a lavish sable coat casually draped over her shoulders, which only partially covered her black leotards and tights while she held a lit cigarette in her left hand. Like Bette Davis in the movie, *All About Eve,* she tossed her coat onto a chair, but it fell to the floor as if it were an incidental old scarf. She didn't bother to pick it up. Instead, still holding the cigarette, she gathered all of us to the center floor to sit in a circle. June straddled a weathered oak stool and spoke to us in a voice pitched not unlike that of a drill sergeant.

"This is a team. There will be no unique, special styles of dancing while you are in this chorus line. When I tell you that your arm and hand should be extended to a specific height at your shoulder or at your waist, I mean just that. One half inch off and I get angry. You are here to work in perfect precision. There will be no arguments amongst you. When you arrive at the theater on videotaping day, I want you dressed as ladies, not looking like tired, over-the-hill and run-of-the-mill chorus dancers with messy hair, no make-up, and sloppy clothes. You will do nothing publicly to embarrass Jackie or me. In addition to the long hard days of rehearsal ahead, you will be expected to take your dance classes and work on your limitations as a dancer. Even if you make it through the first season, you are not guaranteed a position next season. You will audition again. Do not gain weight or you will be fired. Let's get started."

June stepped off the stool setting it aside to review a handful of small, white papers she'd held during her rules-of-engagement talk. These turned out to be notes and drawings, discernible to her alone, that she made during televised football games. June developed dance combinations and patterns utilizing the players' basic formations only to enhance them with her own unique tools of the trade: Dancers, music, lights, cameras, costumes, and vision. She nodded to Peter, her assistant choreographer with a cowboy's weathered face and a muscular body of a world-class athlete. Peter and June both turned to face the floor-to-ceiling mirrored walls. Ignoring us, she demonstrated small, subtle moves to him then asked Peter to 'walk through' the dance combination, which involved limited movement. While I wondered how this understated motion would materialize in any meaningful way, I received my answer. June asked Peter to demonstrate the dance combination in full tempo at performance level. June started our rehearsals at the beginning of each week with a core combination of the new dance routine. Once the first combination's unknown approval code was established, then other dance combinations were developed, discarded, and reincarnated, it seemed, at the speed of light.

Our rehearsal hall for the first season of the show was in the garishly lit basement of the Henry Hudson Hotel where we danced for the marathon audition. The space presented two physical challenges for we were without natural light for most of our waking hours, and the floor upon which we danced was concrete. Dancers and athletes know that when one jumps and lands on concrete it creates whiplash to the spine for there is no 'give' as there would be with wooden flooring. We repeatedly rolled and stretched on the concrete floor with extended arms and legs to create the kaleidoscopic designs for the overhead camera used on videotaping day. Our vertebra protruded from our skeleton-like bodies covered only by a thin layer of skin and a leotard. What this produced by week's end when we were to videotape the show was a succession of bruised and bleeding bones down our spinal columns bandaged for our performance. Fortunately, the cameras were never close enough to capture the little flesh colored Band-Aids that were neatly applied by our wardrobe mistress to each sore and tender backbone.

The scents permeating our rehearsal hall were Jean Naté mixed with a heavy dose of Ben-Gay. Our muscles were sore from the strenuous demands made on our bodies, and we stank from the sweat that poured out of us for eight hours a day, six days a week. I was almost incapable of walking up and down the subway steps in the first weeks for my thighs were not only sore but felt like heavy piano legs. I could not lift them without pain. My plié at the ballet barre, involving my thighs again, was so stiff that I wondered if I would ever be able to reverse it and straighten my legs again. But I loved it all. Each sore muscle and bruise, the challenge of dance combinations I had never seen before, and working with talented, dedicated females. It was surreal for me, and I did believe I was in a waking dream much of the time.

During the long, rigorous days of our rehearsals, there was a one-hour reprieve set aside each week for us to visit the costume designer for fittings. We had an extravaganza of sparkling, colorful costumes with hats and gloves to match. Sometimes we had feathers attached to our hats, or props like umbrellas with crazy-swirls that we spun to create a dizzying effect on camera. My favorite costume was the one we wore for our Christmas show. They were designed to replicate every detail found on little toy soldier dolls with their red, black, and white uniforms accented with gold trim. What made this joyful for me was our makeup. To ensure that we did indeed look like little dolls, each of us spent extra time in make-up applying perfectly round, red-rouged circles on our faces.

On the sixth and final day of our workweek, we had dress rehearsal and then the actual videotaping, generating fourteen to sixteen hours of work in one stretch. We taped our shows at the Ed Sullivan Theater, which encompassed almost an entire city block from West 53rd to West 54th Streets between Broadway and Eighth Avenues. Though our show was the first on CBS to use videotape, we still performed for a live studio audience. There was no canned applause and Jackie needed no canned laughter.

I must admit that even after a long week of strained muscles and a fatigue so intense that I went to bed many nights without eating, the rewards of this sixth day, from dress rehearsal to performance, were my sustenance.

My eyes brimmed with tears the first time, and every time, I heard Jackie's opening theme song, *Melancholy Serenade*. There was a do-or-die thrill for me, a combination of raw nerves and excitement that spread throughout my body when the large, black rolling cameras focused their red lights on us as our dance music struck its first chords. I have been told over the years how fans gathered in their living rooms, certain not to miss our three-minute dance performance. Sammy Spear's Orchestra, live in the studio, played our music, usually Forties or Fifties big-band songs like Glenn Miller's, *In the Mood*. The waves of cheers and applause from the audience grew throughout our demanding routines providing us with even more, precious energy.

I felt the audience's mounting anticipation for the thirty seconds in our routine when we created our intricate floor designs captured with an overhead camera á la Busby Berkeley. And, their excitement was palpable as they waited for the final moment when we rose from the floor quickly assembling to form the kick line that presented a vision of unified precision in a fleeting moment of perceived perfection. Exhilaration and relief engulfed us when our music reached its climax. Our lungs ached for air and sweat streamed down our bodies, soaking our costumes. Yet one more action demanded completion. We formed the well-known split—eight dancers on the left and eight on the right with sixteen pairs of hands extended back towards a glittering red velvet curtain where Jackie made his entrance. The studio audience went wild with applause, yelling when they finally saw this handsome, gentle giant of a man, a man who could make them laugh one second and cry the next.

What I've told you to this point is well known, except for the long rehearsal days, sore muscles, and bleeding backbones. And, in what I've revealed one might think that what we did was the opposite of Camelot. What I am about to tell you is not generally known and was, without doubt, a slice of Camelot.

Jackie loved grandeur, extravagance, and glamour. After every show, sitting at each of our places on the narrow, seventeen-foot dressing table, was a long glossy white box wrapped with a wide, red satin bow. Nestled in this box were one dozen, neatly layered, long-stemmed American Beauty roses. Jackie's generosity was embedded in romanticism and style. He wanted us to exit the theater with our arms filled with flowers. And so, they were there. Every week. Without fail.

My life-long passion for fresh flowers, the subject I've photographed prolifically, is directly related to that ritual Jackie insisted upon. It was a simple gesture touched with class, not unlike his unexpected visits during our long rehearsal days at the hotel.

Jackie could visit us anytime, but when he did, he did it with flair. As he entered the rehearsal hall, at least two waiters with carts of freshly brewed coffee, delicately made pastries, and Champagne followed him. June was never happy about this because of her adamant rule we not gain weight. But, we nibbled and picked and sipped anyway. When we showed Jackie our new routine, the carts were stealthily removed, allowing no further temptations.

The moments of those first weeks, part of my personal tapestry woven nearly outside of time, unfolded into two years. Jackie finally decided to leave New York and do the show from Miami. June was kind enough to ask me if I wanted to join them but said no. I was in the throes of pursuing acting studies and did not want to leave.

And, I had fallen in love.

The Jones Beach Theater at Wantagh, Long Island, New York was, and remains so, a large outdoor amphitheater. June choreographed Broadway musicals and developed musicals from other mediums. We, her dancers, were employed from Memorial Day through Labor Day. In 1963, a musical version of Jules Verne's *Around the World in 80 Days* was produced for the Jones Beach Theater. Musical numbers were written, and dance routines developed. Most of the cast traveled from Manhattan to Wantagh at rush hour in a bus without air conditioning every night. Dom DeLuise, an upcoming comedic actor, sat next to me early in the season. He was a gifted man on many levels. His inherent proclivity for humor made everyone laugh even if he wasn't going for "funny." There was an instant attraction between us, and our conversations ranged through our respective childhoods, our hopes, our insecurities, and everything else. We were never at a loss for words. Eventually, we'd meet in the City to have coffee or ice cream and fell in love.

Dom lived in a place called Hell's Kitchen, located in the 50s off Ninth Avenue. The apartment was a walkup for two or three flights, bright, airy, and usually smelled of Italian cooking. I believe this was a cold-water flat with a bathtub in the kitchen. We also collected empty bottles from the neighbors who left them out for Dom. He was not yet famous and needed the pocket money.

Dom introduced me to the Museum of Modern Art and the Charlie Chaplin film festival playing there for the first time in decades. We saw each film, and Dom's comedic sense was inspired while I learned so much from what he observed and then shared with me. He brought opera into my life as well and taught me about Maria Callas, the voice-of-the century. Her aria, *Memento Mori,* used in the movie, *Philadelphia,* stands the test of time in the rich pathos of her voice. Tom Hanks' rapture as he described Callas' aria to Denzel Washington, Dom demonstrated to me with the same sense of mourning. While I remember Tom Hanks' brilliant performance occurring decades later, I shall never forget the depth of Dom's private presentation in his cold-water flat with a scratchy vinyl record playing as though he were talking to God.

Though poor, Dom still managed to take me to see two groundbreaking events. The first was the film, *Fail Safe,* directed by Sidney Lumet. Dom had a small, pivotal role as the sergeant who unwillingly gives the launch codes to the Russians. Dom could have been an excellent dramatic actor, but his comedy skills were what eventually brought him fame.

The other event was the final preview for *Fiddler on The Roof*. The cast was outstanding with Zero Mostel, a young Bette Midler, and the breathtaking choreography of Jerome Robbins. Dom had seen it several times in standing-room-only but managed to get two seats for us that unforgettable day. There was one dance routine that stopped the show as people stood in a fifteen-minute ovation. I will never forget the resounding applause and cheers as it seemed the bravos would never end. I was awestruck and breathless.

While I did not feel I needed a companion to see Jackie and my dance-sisters leave for Miami, Dom knew better. And I'm grateful for his sensitivity to how finely-tuned I was emotionally.

On August 1, 1964, at the end of my final season as a June Taylor Dancer, Dom and I stood on a humid train platform in Penn Station watching the many people with whom I worked for the past few years board the train to Miami. Jackie hired a band to play on the train for its overnight journey to Florida and, of course, Champagne started flowing for his entourage of one hundred people. As the train began to pull away from the platform and out of the station, I heard the musicians from inside the cars playing *Melancholy Serenade*. I realized a major chapter in my life had irrevocably closed. I was overcome with sadness and turned to Dom sobbing into his broad shoulders.

Perhaps I've rambled on a bit. In my defense, though, there was so much crammed into this period of my life. How could I know history was in the making? Looking at these experiences from the vantage point of present time, I know now that I was a participant in this small, historic moment in our American culture.

Jackie and June are gone. There was an old, grainy YouTube video of the June Taylor Dancers in our opening routine for the launch of the new show in September 1962. It has been removed. All our performances are housed in the Museum of Broadcasting in New York City. There is nothing available to the public that provides a nostalgic snapshot of our dazzling dance routines and costumes. We exist only in the memories of those who remember. My sheer love of dance and forever reaching towards elusive perfection was an act of dedication and love of purpose. We were all *athletes of God*.

The reservoir of moments during those cherished years created an accumulated wealth of tender memories. A weathered oak stool and sable coat belonging to June, and a china teacup and saucer that was Jackie's. Champagne on rolling carts and a large, round black and white wall clock. Long hours of continuous practice in search of perfection, the cause of sore, aching muscles that never seemed to go away. The distinctly different scents between the Ben-Gay of the rehearsal hall and the blend of French perfumes on videotaping day signaling the shift from practice to performance. And, the sweet aroma of red roses given to sixteen female dancers sitting at a long dressing table staring into mirrors applying flawless round, red-rouged circles on their faces.

Jackie was right. It was one hell of a ride and, yes, it was sweet.

May 8

The morning air is bursting with the fresh, clean scent of spring. It seems the buds of every tree and bush opened overnight displaying new green leaves, a lighter shade than they will be in another few weeks. There are many birds in full voice singing their morning praises while Henry sleeps soundly on my desk. Shakespeare finally appears landing on his tree-limb-perch. I'm on my second mug of tea as I sit in front of the computer thinking about Dom. I cannot leave that open-ended. There was an ending for us and one that many people have experienced at least once.

Days after the train departed for Miami, Dom was hired to be a regular on the new Carol Burnett television show, and from there he was launched into stardom. I was awarded another seventeen weeks at the Copa as opening act for more well-known stars.

Not unexpectedly, we reached a point in our relationship that it would either go forward, or end. Ours had been an innocent puppy love that lasted from early summer through late autumn of 1964. Dom wanted me to live with him. My mother reminded me of my Catholicism and that I was to remain a virgin until I married. Dom was not prepared for marriage with his career about to skyrocket, and I wasn't either. He took mom out to lunch to try and persuade her that he loved me and would care for me even though we were unmarried. Whatever she said in their conversation that caused Dom to leave me I do not know. What followed was heartbreaking for both of us. Dom called to break off our romance. He was gentle, kind, and tearful. I understood why he wanted an adult relationship with a woman, so our sweet season of love ended.

Dom eventually married actress, Carol Arthur. They were married forty years, maybe more, producing three talented sons. I pray Dom died a happy man. A loving, devoted wife and three sons who act and direct and produce had to be a good part of the joy he wanted in life. He loved deeply, and I know he was deeply loved, not only by his family but by all the hearts he touched through his work.

While the sting of Dom leaving me left a deeper hole than anyone knew, an occurrence at the Copa that season, softened my heartbreak. Tony Bennett was the star of our show for two weeks. During my performance, he stood on the balcony leading down to the small stage and watched every night. I knew he was studying me with his kind, smiling eyes. One night, our show's director came to the ladies' dressing room and announced that Tony would like to talk to me as I was escorted into his dressing room. Tony explained that a new technology called cable television had been launched in closed circuit format within the finer New York hotels. He asked me if I would join him in an interview. I was shocked and said, "What do I say?" He said there would be an interviewer and not to be nervous for he would be sitting next to me. I forgot the specific questions asked of Tony and me, but I do remember one, which was, "Please tell us why you dance?" I couldn't just say *because I like it*. Tony took my hand and answered for me saying, "Lee Anne's soul is what drives her abilities. She glows with it, and I watch the audience respond to this young woman who overflows with talent and has no idea how she touches our hearts and souls." I was speechless. If I knew then what I *would* know several decades later, I'd have treated my talents as blessings rather than good fortune, or luck.

August 27

It is early dawn and the air is already heavy with humidity. A sultry day arrives. It is also my sixty-first birthday. I made no plans. Not this year. What is sixty-one? Not a milestone. Anna and Peddler called wanting to celebrate, but the sole focus of my life has been on the photos, now complete, and the wax and oil paintings waiting for their final review before I say they are finished, step back, and release them. Though art is not a biological birth, it is a birth nonetheless, the exposure of one's soul to the world if there is truth in the work.

Immediately following Labor Day, I conclude a consulting assignment I somehow managed to thread through these summer months. Gratefully, it was in Syracuse, and I was able to drive there and back most of the time with only a few overnights. Arthur and I were well compensated, and this replenished my bank account since the consulting practice was slow this year.

I'll set up the grill for a rib-eye steak on bone accompanied with a side salad of garden tomatoes and greens. I'd love a glass of Champagne, although I'd really prefer a vodka martini, my former drink of choice. It is disturbing to me after these accumulated years of sobriety that I would think of alcohol, no less at dawn. But I feel wound up and spinning for these are the moments I most enjoyed drinking, although never in the morning. When I go to the studio, I'll take an iced tea to acknowledge my completed artwork scheduled to exhibit in a gallery near Woodstock for several months beginning late September.

Henry has changed, or perhaps mellowed. He comes to the studio, and he frequently arrives home from his adventures in the evenings. He's around me more, staying out for shorter periods of time. Henry is five years old and I see no signs of illness other than his attaching himself to me in more intimate ways than what was his nature to do. I wonder what Shakespeare does when I'm absent? I think about this now, for I have another month-long photo shoot in Maine. I leave September 29.

August 28

I must resume writing if only to turn from what has become pressure to something that brings calm. I've had no time, nor did I try to create a schedule, to continue with the narrative. I allowed the immediate deadline work to dominate my life this past little while.

I wrote many pages back that there were choices, paths taken and others not in one's journey. My life changed at twenty-three due to a very deliberate, willful decision.

I continued to work in television and radio commercials, had another gig or two at the Copa, and several summer stock performances, most notably *Annie Get Your Gun,* starring the beautiful Lee Remick. I was the ingénue with new song and dance numbers I was asked to choreograph. So, this was an opportunity to place a choreographer credit on my resume.

We traveled the east coast and the best summer stock theaters because Lee was the new movie star of the day and deservedly so. She was also generous, unassuming, and worked hard. Who knew she had a big singing voice?

Years later, Stephen Sondheim discovered her vocal talent and cast her in the musical, *Follies,* singing *Anyone Can Whistle.* Perfect for Lee. Her hair was true strawberry blond framing ever-so-pale blue eyes, and a nose sprinkled with a few well-placed freckles on fair, porcelain skin. Her beauty was real from the inside, and out. Her children were mirror images of her, and they joined her off and on throughout the summer. Lee and I were excited when Irving Berlin, age ninety-nine, came to see our performance at Old Westbury on Long Island. Lee Remick died an early death at fifty-six, and I mourned the loss of this talented, gracious woman.

My passion for performing was rapidly fading away. I met my first husband, Tom, during a modeling job at the Coliseum in New York. I was twenty-three and rapidly tiring of audition after audition, finding less and less performance work. I was war-weary from years of my young life invested into something I loved. The reality? I lost the willingness, the ache required for the continuous study and hard work. At only twenty-three, I had already worked for sixteen years.

Tom was Jewish. And, he was eye-candy for most women. He was tall, muscular, black wavy hair, skin the color of a perpetual suntan, brown-black eyes, and intelligently witty. When we were just dating, my mom had no problems. She worked in an office but continued living with me. I asked her to move out many times, but she refused. Tom and I had a rapid romance of three months and decided to marry as soon as possible.

Mom was enraged, and I was soon to discover that she could not face the reality of living alone. So much so, she checked into a hotel with a case of scotch, saying she was going to jump from the top floor and kill herself if I married Tom. She was not anti-Semitic like dad but thought I was making an enormous mistake in judgment. Moreover, I was abandoning her. "Who will oversee your theater career?" I knew I no longer needed her. I not only outgrew her endless critiques but decided to end my performance career. I called dad. I called Tom. And, I called my closest friend, April. Once dad arrived from Ohio, we sat together in the studio apartment, and he took the reins, called the hotel, and got the police. He brought her home. There was no scotch found. Not this time.

If I believed the sheer decision to bring closure to my performance career was indeed the end, it was not. The real climax was the follow-up argument with my mother and the reckless action taken on my part. Tom and I arrived at the apartment to retrieve items I needed. Mom raged on and on at both of us how this marriage was doomed because of religion, different lifestyles, and my precious, *precious* work toward stardom. A savage fury manifested within me fueled by years of mom's systematic, psychological abuse.

I entered our large walk-in closet and threw everything that had anything to do with my performance career down the incinerator just across the hall. I stuffed the chute with dance shoes, costumes, music scores, and the watercolor paintings of unique Copa costumes made especially for me. There were scrapbooks of reviews from performances, black and white photography shots for auditions, and even my work-out clothes. I burned everything I could find just as my father had done with my first stories. Tears spilled from Tom's eyes as he tried to stop me. Nothing had the power to prevent me from this brutal assault on my mother. I wanted her to be witness to the end of her dreams for me. She was horrified and finally silent. Upon our leaving, the walls shook when she slammed the door shut.

Tom and I eloped one month later. Mom did not speak to me for two years. I was twenty-three when I ended my performance career. I wanted a husband, home, anything that would take me away from the tyranny of my mother.

I never again performed on stage, or theater, or television. I even stopped taking dance and acting classes. Do I have regrets? No. Do I miss it? No. One needs to have an absolute yearning inside to perform or engage in any type of artistic endeavor. Without that ache, we repeat our work, and it becomes lifeless reducing it to pablum. I lost that hunger. And the many years devoted to professional performance and study stopped. It was abrupt and absolute.

September 29

 I left the cabin at 5 A.M. Henry was there in time for his saucer of milk and Anna will stay the month while I journey through a specific area of Maine. Today's goal is to arrive at my destination before sunset. This presents many miles to drive in one day and I'm in need of breakfast! Once I'm on the Mass Pike, I will take a short detour off a little-known-exit that leads to one of those authentic diners where professional waitresses, without fail, visit tables with freshly brewed coffee, anticipating and scanning for each customer's need. One doesn't raise a hand or make a verbal request. They just know. They are among those who make what they do an art-form. The platters of wholegrain pancakes with fresh blueberries and real maple syrup are mythic. Upon leaving, they will fill my thermos with hot, black coffee. They are only twenty minutes more, and I can smell the hearty roast coffee even now.

 It is mid-October, and the autumnal display of foliage in the Berkshires is an extravaganza of colors consisting of rich sienna, yellow, gold, bright orange, dazzling red. Moreover, a flawless blue-sky offsets nature's presentation. Surely the Creator is showing off today.

 My designation is Deer Isle, an island off the upper mid-coast of Maine. It is a long drive, one in which I usually stop overnight in Kennebunkport. This time I decided to drive straight through to wake in the morning to the sound of ocean waves, either lapping or pummeling Maine's rugged shoreline, depending on the weather.

I enjoy long drives. There is freedom to stop and go as I please and think about nothing or muse about the state of the world. I play my favorite tunes, listen to audiobooks, and daydream. Presently my mind indulges in a long-time dream to drive across country and back. I'd plan a northern route going, and a southern return. It is frivolous to entertain this dream for there is no time in my life, as it is currently arranged, to embark on such a long journey. I've read and re-read Steinbeck's, *Travels with Charley,* and I'm always there with them, savoring each moment. Wistfully, I fold the dream like a piece of yellow, worn paper, and place it into a file titled DREAMS AND WISHES, residing in the farthest corner of my mind. I'll retrieve this file again, as I've done many times in the past, to do a pulse check on my life. The question is, am I living the life I truly want to live? And, what does that life consist of and look like? This is too much to think about now. Also, I am ravenous. Only ten minutes more.

I turn my attention to more immediate things as I mentally run through my planned stops to Deer Isle to buy food and other essentials. Wiscasset for homemade bread, Damariscotta for the world's best sticky buns and a giant cup of French press dark roast coffee, Kennebunkport for lunch at Mabel's Lobster Claw, maybe Belfast, then Bucksport (the final stop for staples).

I know where to obtain what I need. Albeit for this trip, I require more for it is not one week's work, but an entire month to do a photo shoot of areas of Acadia National Park, various harbors and boats, and the Schoodic Peninsula. Writing will accompany the photos, but I admit to exhaustion, and an unidentifiable inner restlessness I can't seem to shake. I mentioned it when we memorialized my sister, Lily. The unease remains. Sometimes it is in the forefront of my mind, and at others it is an echo that never leaves.

Arthur brought me to Maine, specifically Deer Isle, as he did the Florida paradise. And, as I did with the Island, I continued vacationing in Maine off and on following our divorce. Arthur liked out-of-the-way places, journeys off known pathways. He lives his life this way, and I was beneficiary of his penchant for wanderlust.

As co-owner and founding partner of a successful boutique management consultancy, Arthur and I worked hard to build our business. Painstaking, challenging work was not an unknown to either of us. Initially, just the two of us managed to build a client roster of significant marketers that read like a list of Blue Bloods. I am no longer in the office and telecommute most of the time. But, I did enjoy working with our employees and managing their career growth when I was a full-time partner. I still receive satisfaction in the personal relationships I've built over the years with our marketing clients and their advertising agencies. Admittedly, I am proud of the attention accorded us, and I love making money.

I arrive at the diner and am famished! Coffee is immediately poured. I'll use this time for cell phone calls and email replies and then get back on the road. I hope there are no fires to put out at the cabin or the office.

Everything was running smoothly at the office, and my plans and stops flowed like a well-choreographed dance routine. After listening to a variety of boring radio stations, I played my own tunes, a mixture of Bruce Springsteen, Yo-Yo Ma, and *La Boheme.*

With only a half hour more of non-stop driving, I do so in silence taking in the tall pines of Maine, smelling new scents in the air. Thirty-five minutes later, I arrive at the cottage.

The sun is setting upon my approach, though the long dirt road leading to the rental is a challenge with its ruts and rocks. Typical Maine. I step out of the truck and walk to the edge of the great lawn overlooking the craggy coastline, tall pines, and the Atlantic Ocean. Inhaling the salt air, I am soothed at the sight and sound of pure white gulls, and breathe out a long exhale, hearing a sole, plaintive foghorn emanating from Stonington Harbor. Within minutes, the weariness of the long drive drifts away.

The cottage I rented as my base for the month is not a large dwelling, but it faces the ocean with woodland protecting it from any sites or sounds other than what is near—ocean pounding ancient rocks, gulls screeching, birds of many varieties soaring through the trees and above the waters, and the occasional harbor sounds and ship bells as the lobstermen and women leave Stonington early morning.

I step on to a covered porch with large floor-to-ceiling mullioned wavy-glass windows and French entrance doors, all providing ocean views. The key is in a small metal box behind the woodpile (this is Maine and not New York City, so the little, hidden box is enough), and, thankfully, the caretaker left the porch light on.

As I enter the living room, I'm taken aback at its austere decor. There are only a few necessary items. A loveseat, rocker, and an over-stuffed chair. A hooked rug sits in front of the small loveseat, and a colonial pine chest placed on top of the small carpet is the coffee table. There are a few antique lamps, a large, empty bookcase with drawers, and gratefully, a new Vermont Castings wood stove with an ample supply of wood and kindling set aside with more on the porch. The stove was stacked by the caretaker with kindling and wood. I just need to light a match.

I survey the kitchen surprised at the extent of cookware and utensils containing more than enough for my cooking needs. I planned simple soups, fish and salad, and eggs and toast for breakfast. I brought my own teapot for brewing tea in the mornings and for those times a strong cup of dark roast coffee is needed, a French press. I finally look around and take in the whole room.

It is a replica of the living room and not unexpected given previous Maine rental experiences. It is sparse, with a square, rustic pine table and chairs. There is a large stainless sink and an antique Garland gas stove. Everything is spotless, though, along with some chipped plates and mugs.

A freshly baked blueberry pie sits on the countertop covered with a red-checkered napkin. How thoughtful. Gracious too.

Dinner is done once I unpack for I will have pie and tea in front of the wood stove. The temperature has dropped to the low-thirties. There is a chill in the air, and I love it.

I walk from the living room through a small hallway to the master bathroom and bath. This too is simple but has everything I need, including lovely crisp white bed linens and down-feathered pillows and duvet. A deep claw-foot tub resides in the bathroom next to a window overlooking what I believe are perennial gardens.

There are small plug-in heaters in the bathroom and bedroom, and to my delight, two sliding glass doors lead out to a sizeable porch with an ocean view. The porch contains only one Adirondack rocker, footstool, and a small end table. All the rooms are somewhat bare, yet everything one could need is here. Though there is no cell tower, there is a telephone landline for my use. And, the owner brought in his own Internet via cable. How very expensive to do and I am grateful he did.

I head for a hot bath and slip into my flannel pajamas. I unpack a box of books, knitting projects for Christmas, my Bose radio, and CDs. There is no TV. Not a problem. I cut a large slice of pie and make a small pot of tea.

I walk to the living room and wood fire, sit on the shabby love seat, which is quite comfortable despite my earlier misgivings, and wallow in the homemade pie and tea. Once sated, I look around the room with more attention.

The walls, utterly stark without any attempt at decoration, are pine as are the wide-planked floorboards. Some beams appear to be hand-hewn, so the cottage is most likely early 1900s. This room, though sorely bereft of personality, is reminiscent of most vintage Maine summer camps. 'Camps' are what these rustic cottages were called in the day. Humble in adornment, stunning views with large lawns leading down to rocky shores, and an abundance of old money to support the upkeep.

Though it is nearing ten-thirty, I put another log on the wood stove fire, plump up the pillows, and cover my lap with an old hand-stitched quilt of many colors.

I miss Henry. Usually, he would be out at this hour. When I left the cabin this morning, he walked out with me, paused and looked over his shoulder, and then walked on into the woods. I saw Shakespeare and waved goodbye as he sat quite still.

I brought many books, but I want to complete Sue Monk Kidd's, *The Secret Life of Bees*.

September 30

I wake up on the sofa and see that it is two o'clock in the morning. There is only a small bed of coals in the wood stove, so I stoke them and pack the stove tight with wood. Like my cabin, this will ensure warmth in the morning and a hardy bed of coals upon which to pile larger logs. The book had slipped off my lap to the floor. I earmarked the page I last read with non-sleepy eyes, left it on the sofa, and plunged into the bed, listening to the waves lap against the shoreline.

When I woke again, I found the morning brought with it a pea-soup fog, one where you can't see but a foot ahead. Surrendering to the cold, damp day, I slip on my gray baggy sweats, an olive-green turtleneck sweater, and a gray sweatshirt over that. Layering is the secret to comfort in Maine.

I am not yet hungry for breakfast after last night's pie. So, with a hot mug of tea in hand and my laptop open, I continue my story. It is a confession of a decision made, a piece of my life concealed in the dark recesses of my memory. I didn't sleep well, and it wasn't the long drive or the tasty blueberry pie. I thought I dreamt about Lily. But, no, I dreamt about my baby. I have no children, but I was pregnant. Only once.

They called it a miscarriage, but I deliberately traveled at a precarious time in my pregnancy for a demanding consulting assignment in Indianapolis. I was in my first trimester and there was a little blood from time-to-time. I ignored the doctor's request for me to stay at home for a few weeks. Instead, I drove to a dozen or more retail outlets on a day registering 104 degrees. I defied my doctor's advice to stay home for I felt strong, healthy, and believed I was Superwoman.

After hours of driving through the heat, getting in and out of my rental car to make my assessments of the retail stores in question, something moved in my lower abdomen and sunk. The car seat, my clothes, my legs, and shoes were covered in blood. After cleaning myself up and changing clothes in a diner where they politely ignored all the blood-stained clothes I wore when I first entered, I caught an earlier flight home, realizing I lost my baby. The car service driver I always requested, took one look at my ghostly white face with sunken eyes, and made haste to the emergency room at Mt. Sinai. I was only okay upon examination, for I had lost a lot of blood. The miscarriage was confirmed. And I was both sad and relieved.

Surely, I did nothing wrong. I was busy, stressed, and building a business. While I could've foregone that business trip and considered more bed rest, my work took precedence over everything, even the life growing inside of me. So, I gambled. If the baby survived, wonderful. I was in-between marriages. While I knew the father, for I had been seeing him nine or ten months, I had no intentions of marrying him. I would've been a single mom and could easily afford whatever was needed. I convinced myself, nonetheless, that the miscarriage was the best resolution. I was so persuasive that I thoroughly deceived myself. This is an uncomfortable, painful memory. Am I deluding you? Or, am I masking a deeper truth about myself I find lamentable?

The kitchen table is the only convenient place to work. I had hoped to lay out a workspace in the living room near the wood stove. However, it's good for me to break up my time sitting at the computer, stand up and walk to stoke the bed of coals and add fresh logs. Once back in the kitchen, I close the laptop because I'm finally hungry. I make coffee, scramble farm fresh eggs and toast a thick slice of homemade sourdough bread. Once I plunge the coffee in the French press, I'll slather sweet cream butter on the toast, add some local honey and place it all on a large butler's tray found on top of the refrigerator and head for the living room to eat in front of the fire. Still, there is only fog outside my window views.

I'm a fire-storm of thoughts and memories. This eerie fog, the inability to do what I came here to accomplish has made me fidgety. Remembering my own lost baby, and Lily's ceremony in the tepee, I've begun second-guessing my decisions. I've always felt a bit bewildered about my free-spirited friends, Anna and Peddler. That confusion has increased. It may be envy for their courage, or my fear of something nettlesome and thorny in my flesh and in my soul. Are these issues related? I believe they are yet I fail to see a clear connection.

There will be no photo shoot today unless the fog burns away, which I doubt. Before I start writing, I pour another cup of coffee with a dollop of cream. But, the words do not come. The page remains blank. I need time to think about this darkness that stalks me. I would like to take a long walk, but the fog still rolls along the ground. No, no, no! I left the snake stick at the cabin and I'll be walking and hiking extensively. Oh well. The wood stove needs a couple of thick, big logs and the damper lowered while I'm out. I pack my laptop in its case, deciding to bring it along. Out I go in layered clothing, hiking boots, and a laptop.

I walk about a mile and come across a high outcropping overlooking the ocean.

The fog is not dense here as I spot a suggestion of shoreline. I hear the Stonington Harbor foghorn and breathe in the salt air. I needed the air as well as the walk. I zip open the laptop case to begin my notes and with any luck write a few lines, if not a page. I need to quiet myself first, so with eyes closed, I sit on the rock listening to sounds. I look at the clock on my computer and realize I've been here for two hours. Two hours? I fell asleep and that's unusual for me. I need to go into Stonington for a bowl of clam chowder and buy haddock to bake for dinner.

Stonington is one of the last authentic lobster fishing villages on our east coast. I found new shops, among them an excellent liquor store, bought more provisions, and a bottle of wine. I saw a particularly expensive and rare vintage bottle of a California Chardonnay. All the fire alarms went off in my head. My hands shook, and my heart thumped in my ears like a bass drum.

Returning from Stonington, I felt an ominous darkness following me, but I shrugged it off. *Come on, Lee Anne, you never drank that much. You had a few martinis at night. This is only wine. Just wine.*

Once back at the cottage, I head for the wood stove like a lemming. Wood stoves require attention and artistic care. I make outstanding wood fires. I learned from Dave and then years on my own at the cabin. I stoke the coals, turn small logs, and add more. All is well now with the nurturing heat of the stove. In the kitchen, I conduct preliminary preparation for dinner of salad fixings, potatoes, and chill the Chardonnay along with a crystal wine glass I found in the cabinets. All I must do when I'm hungry is bake the haddock. It doesn't get better than this. It's only four o'clock and the niggling thoughts about babies, freedom, Blue Highway dreams, have not stopped. They are ever-present specters now. I've made thorough notes on the laptop about this day, the wine, the darkness pressing in, and the specters. I'm ready to return to my book.

October 15

I write this in the evening. We expect a hard frost tonight. I love the cold, even the long dark days accompanying it. I am not afraid of a dark room, or that caused by the winter season. I fear darkness that consumes the soul.

These past weeks have been filled with the rigor of hiking, carrying photography equipment, and witnessing the splendor of Acadia National Park and Mt. Desert.

I lost my way on one of the carriage paths, cleared wide enough in the early 1900s for the wealthy New York and Boston patrons to ride their carriages and horses through Acadia. Today these smooth, easily walked paths are covered with finely ground stone. Somehow, I found myself tangled into a figure-eight pathway that unraveled up and down to the point I couldn't find my way out.

I was already tired, following a lengthy photo shoot of the remarkable Witch Hole Pond site where the Pond, more like a small lake, offers a clear mirrored reflection of everything surrounding it, including small butterflies. Each time I thought I solved the figure-eight, I was on yet another new path. The sun was almost behind the horizon. Dusk was about to descend and I no longer passed people along the way. Even after my years at the cabin, I was more than concerned for Acadia is a wildlife park. An old man with a knotted cane, not unlike a smaller version of Peddler, recognized I had a deer-caught-in-headlights look in my eyes. Though he said little, he was kind and walked with me to the proper descent. I thanked him, saying I was grateful. He nodded, said nothing, and headed back up the mountain. Another angel.

I exited the Park precisely where my car was parked but could barely move. Memories of the first days as a June Taylor dancer surfaced with surprising realism. My body was a mass of stiffness and aching muscles. Everywhere. What was I thinking? I am not nineteen. I am sixty-one. A healthy, active sixty-one, but this was a lesson in the limitations and acceptance of a different pace I need to respect in this season of my life.

I stopped at a restaurant and without thinking, or hesitation of any kind, ordered and quickly consumed a vodka martini, then lobster with a baked potato and sour cream, biscuits and butter, a second martini, and finally a rich chocolate mousse cake. I felt much better. The Power Bars while hiking did not do the job. This meal renewed my soul! And, to my surprise so did the vodka. I felt free again. I loved every sip of it.

Tomorrow I journey to a place untouched by the hands-of-time. The Schoodic Peninsula.

October 16

We are cloaked in fog this morning and I will not be visiting Schoodic. Moreover, Arthur called with a work matter involving the writing of a proposal for a new client. A proposal! They are arduous. We usually co-write our recommendations, but he's preparing a final report for another client. Because of fog and worldly-work, I did not see the outdoors until mid-afternoon when the heavy mist finally lifted revealing ocean and landscape.

I completed the draft proposal and emailed it to the office staff for those illusive misspellings and typos. However, I am pleased that the day for creative work is not lost. Once free to leave my laptop, I walk outside into the sunlight and stroll onto a narrow road where paths branch off into woodlands. I am not on the trail for long when what I think is an apparition is, in fact, a large empty boat hull secluded in a woodland graveyard. I take several views of the shell, imagining its secrets and tall tales to tell. How did it get into these deep woodlands? I am satisfied with what I captured through my lens and head back to the main road and cottage.

Once back, I take note of the active fire blazing in the wood stove, go to the kitchen and make a martini on the rocks. Three olives. I sit in front of the fire taking small sips staring at the logs burn. I feel better about the day, the proposal, and that I was able to photograph something of merit. I heat up left-over lentil soup with a small plate of olive oil dip for the warm, crusty baguette, and fixed my second drink.

I think about plans for venturing to the Schoodic Peninsula tomorrow. I also think about my inner restlessness, drinking again, and babies never born.

October 17

Dense fog. Again. I have no choice. I need to push on with this project. These were the conditions in which I drive to the Schoodic Peninsula. Only ten percent of the visitors to Acadia National Park take the extra hour to reach this part of this remarkable national park. If heaven exists, then part of it is in Schoodic.

It's a bleak drive north on Route 1 and onto 186 through Winter Harbor, taking more than an hour. The fog's mist is heavy enough that windshield wipers are needed, though it's not raining. Am I crazy? What do I hope my camera can accomplish in this weather?

It had been twenty years since my last visit to Schoodic. I'm apprehensive regarding my return, for I believed Schoodic would have to be different as everything, in each moment, continues to change. Still, I hope every aspect of Schoodic will be exactly as I remembered.

Schoodic has a Scenic Byway, which is a one-way road that loops around and out back to the main road. When I first entered Schoodic twenty years earlier, it was in torrential rain. I saw nothing, but this dark, single lane road enveloped by pine trees on both sides. Then the vista opened, and there was no one, not a soul to be seen, except for hundreds of seagulls flying and landing in the rain on the large flat rock formations that are, quite simply, the rocks-of-time, perhaps even eternity.

Some 'thing,' perhaps an illusion, but I think not, changed the still-point within me. There was a holiness present. The vast ocean pounding ancient rock formations, salt water on my face and hands, and gulls at peace in their habitat. Standing alone amidst all the natural wonderment clarified, for a moment, where we mortals stand, so small, and yet exceptional in Creation. *Powerfully and wonderfully made just slightly lower than the angels, and yet a mere breath in the vastness of eternity.* Yes, words and fragments of Psalms flowed into my heart.

As I enter Schoodic today, I am flooded with these memories and inwardly smile at the first of many images and scenes from twenty years ago. My heart soars with excitement as I wend my way to the rocks-of-time.

Schoodic's character is raw and rugged and pure. Rock formations along its shoreline present a rare poetic vision. It offers a broad plateau of pink and red stone that glaciers carved, and ocean waves continue to smooth. The rocks sit as architectural monuments to Creation. When Thomas Cole produced his first paintings of Mount Desert, the critics in New York lambasted his work, saying that everyone knew the rocks on Maine's coastline were gray, not red, or of other hues. Cole was right. The critics were wrong.

The seagulls are an inspirational living force of the Schoodic landscape. At first glance, one is staggered by the hundreds of white gulls gathered in one place. They love to perform too as they strut, bathe, and pose for my camera while the fog weaves its way around the rocks and crannies, lifting, then blanketing us once more. The mist plays with me, as do the gulls, and I ask, "Do you remember me? Do you?" I step carefully over the slippery rocks back to the truck to begin my journey around the single-lane road. Yet I stop one more time to take a picture of a shimmering mist, almost alive, weaving in and out of an eerie bog.

Once off the by-way, I feel relief, exhilaration, and exhaustion. I head south on Route 1. There's a message on my cell once back into an area where there are cell towers. Arthur has edits for me. The tyrannical project was waiting for my return. I am chilled, and visibility is now greatly diminished as the fog's density increases. Time to return to Stonington.

Ensconced at the cottage, I fill the wood stove and make a pot of tea. I stoically settle into what I believe is an arduous task, only to find that the writing proceeds smoothly, and with Arthur's blessing, the proposal is complete. He asks if I visited Schoodic and I report that nothing changed. He is happy for me, knowing I took memorable images, especially one that would become an homage to Thomas Cole. As a collector of the Hudson River School of Painting, which Cole founded, Arthur is thrilled.

I make my martini and start dinner preparations. Pasta primavera tonight. There is satisfaction in completing a challenging journey and a creatively productive day. *Show me the work of my hands.* Another Psalm fragment. And, yes, today my hands feel blessed.

October 18

Henry is dead.

He came to me in a dream last night walking toward me with his long, sinewy stride offering his head and ears for a scratch and the soft stroke of my hand. He purred the whole time. I thought it amazing Henry followed me to Maine from our cabin. I couldn't fathom how he did this. I finally wake and see it is three o'clock in the morning. Though only a dream, I am cold with fear that Henry indeed came to say goodbye. There was a prescient quality to the dream. It was disturbing and remains so.

I adopted Henry over five years ago merely to keep the cabin free of mice. He was feral, born somewhere in the heavily wooded lands of the Catskill State Park. His mother died while weaning him. A woman discovered him on a trail hike, trying to draw milk from his dead mother, took him home, and nursed him back into life and health until he was four months old. However, she already had many cats and was eager to find another home for this kitten. Since I wanted a good hunter for my cabin, it was a perfect match of timing and circumstance.

At four months of age, Henry was tall, already strapping, and elegantly handsome. His nature was inherently sweet and gentle, causing me to wonder if he would be a good hunter because of his kind demeanor. His golden eyes, even at this early age, reflected wisdom—a quiet knowing and acceptance of things. I watched him hunt and observed his muscular frame develop into something akin to a world-class athlete. As he matured his wisdom deepened, and I believed he knew more, cared more, and was finely tuned to the wildness and mystery of his natural world, as well as to us mere humans.

Henry was often found sleeping in the sun behind the juniper bushes at the backside of the cabin. He slept peacefully yet ever alert. The subtlest change in his environment would disrupt his snooze and cause him to immediately focus his senses to discern whether a sound, rustle of a leaf, or flutter of something required his full attention. Of the many photos I took of Henry, there is one I cherish most. He is stretched out flicking his tale observing the world from under an old pine bench, an ideal shelter from the hot summer sun.

I knew something was different about Henry when I left for Maine. It was that last pause and glance over his shoulder as I departed the cabin that troubled me. Now I understand. Henry knew these were the final moments we would see each other. Call it my imagination, or silliness. Dismiss my feelings. But Henry and I were bonded. He knew he would not see me again and now I know he is no more.

I wrap myself in a quilt, sit on the porch, and listen to the ocean as I try to calm my breath and meditate. It's too early for me to call Anna. I wait. Looking up at a dark sky, small snowflakes begin to fall. As I enter the cottage, I note the wood stove pumping heat, so I go to the kitchen and put on the kettle for tea.

I call Anna from the landline at 6:00 A.M. I cannot wait any longer. She picks up on the second ring. Before Anna could say anything, I asked, "Anna, is everything okay?"

"Lee Anne, I tried calling just a few days ago to say that Henry disappeared for more than a week." Her voice, low and husky, used carefully measured words. I reply, "Oh, don't worry, he's probably out for a long adventure." However, I knew Henry was dead. Anna was silent for what seemed an eon, then said, "No, Lee Anne, Peddler found him in the woods. He died under a hemlock tree. He was not in a fight. There were no marks on him, just a drop of blood beneath his nose. Shakespeare was watching over him. Peddler thinks it was an aneurysm. He lay as if he were sleeping peacefully. What do you want us to do?" I tremble and freeze despite the warm stove and blanket. I try to breathe normally, but am only able to gasp brief, shallow breaths. I can't get enough air into my lungs, and a full-blown panic attack is upon me.

"Hello? Lee Anne?"

I ask, "Where is he? What did Peddler do?"

"Don't worry. Peddler retrieved him and is keeping Henry safe. What do you want us to do?"

Oh, my boy, my muse, my other heartbeat.

Rage surges through my veins and with a voice like a snarling growl, I answer, "What to do? You're asking me what to do? The only thing that can be done. Cremate him. Don't wait for me. I am not strong enough to see his vibrant body lifeless, and I have even less courage to witness a cremation. But, please, *please* tell Peddler not to keep any part of him. Do you understand?" Silence. "Do you understand me? It would not be a present for me. Leave nothing of Henry. Keep his ashes safe. I'll start for home today."

I know Anna sensed from my tone that things were not right with me, and not just due to Henry's death. I chose not to tell her I started drinking again. I say goodbye, walk to the refrigerator, take the vodka from the freezer, and then put it back. I always prided myself on not being a morning or day drinker. *Yet who am I deceiving?*

I quickly pack fast and leave the cottage by 8 A.M. I haven't eaten. I already vomited several times. I want to be at the cabin now. *Now!* I am irrational and should not drive. But I drive with the goal of reaching home by midnight. And while I drive, tears and memories flow as they always do when one loses a precious soul in life.

My most vivid and haunting memory of Henry emerged from a tangle of emotions. It was from an early period in our history together.

He was six months old when he engaged in an adventure, or perhaps drama is more appropriate, that remains engraved in the folds of my memories.

It was an uncommonly warm, sixty-degree February day. And it was the day of Henry's memorable hunt. Though, snow still prevailed at our mountaintop cabin. An indigo blue sky reigned over the land, showcasing the pristine snow with a bright, almost blinding sun, shining through the bare branches of tall trees. This was an early taste of spring, and the ease of walking around outdoors without layers of clothing was unadulterated freedom. A thick, wool shirt and turtleneck was enough.

Henry was out on an excursion, while Shakespeare and I took a long walk in the afternoon, soaking up the warmth and the sunlight. When I returned, it was time to feed Henry his evening meal of canned food. This is how I trained him not to wander off so that he returned each evening for this meal and every morning for his milk. However, Henry was not to be seen. I put the food out anyway, confident he would eventually show up.

And he did. With great steadfastness, he climbed the steep, long stone steps to the front porch holding something substantial in his mouth. Within moments, I realized it was a small grouse. It had speckled, brown, black, and white feathers, and was large for Henry at only six-months to drag. But he did.

This catch of Henry's was against the law of nature and too impossible even for him to accomplish. How could he possibly catch a grouse or a small owl at his age? I had never heard of a cat catching an owl. In fact, quite the opposite.

But, no, it was a good-sized bird that he dragged unto the patchy snow-covered grass as he played with its limp body. Then, abruptly, he left it and sought his food on the porch. Soon after his canned meal was finished, I watched him in the snow, dancing a cat ballet over his prey. Surely this death-dance was primal in its roots and a form of celebration. He clawed, rolled, played and studied his kill. He stopped for a while, cleaned himself, and then resumed his ritual dance. I observed this ceremony with fascination as well as disgust. And to my dismay, Henry joined me on the porch during one of his breaks and looked at me with such pride.

We sat together, never too close in the early years, for Henry insisted that a respectful distance was maintained. With my light scratching behind his ears and the symphonic purr of Henry's response, I said goodnight to him and went inside. I turned off the porch lights and wrestled with the mixed feelings I had regarding this killing.

Henry did what is in his nature to do. Nevertheless, he slaughtered this mysterious, unidentifiable bird creature, this other being. I was not angry with Henry, but I was unsettled at the sight of him dancing his dance in preparation of what I believed would be the final mutilation of the bird. It was sobering.

I tried to read before I went to sleep but failed. My mind was active with thoughts, stuff, things. I was concerned about the bloody remains of the creature. I knew that cats leave something of their killing, as Henry almost always did with mice and chipmunks, and his catch was usually left half-eaten. I resolved to have Hank, due to perform chores, remove whatever was left of the creature the next day. With a plan in place, I finally fell asleep.

It rained all night, a heavy, pounding rain, so my sleep was fitful. I finally surrendered to waking up and entered my day. It was 5 A.M. Apart from the persistent, hard rain, this was usually my quiet, still time. But this morning was neither silent nor still. I heard loud vocalizations from Henry, a rhythmic, chanting sound. Really? Not possible. As I approached the front door, I had renewed thoughts of his killing on my mind, which conjured visions of Henry covered with the creature's innards as pieces of flesh hung from his fur, half dried and half still moist.

The bird would be spread open in some ghoulish way, no longer identifiable as it was reduced to something raw and hideous. Its once-greatness as a living creature, would be demeaned entirely and lost forever. I switched the porch lights on with some hesitancy and looked through the oval glass window of the entrance door. Though I thought I heard Henry, he was nowhere to be seen. In his stead, on the doormat, an offering was left for me, the remains of Henry's hunt from the previous day. It was not the whole killing half-eaten, but something much more. Something derived from sorcery itself. It was not anything I could imagine or fictionalize for a story.

I knew that when cats caught feathered prey, they would pluck their killing first of its feathers and those feathers would be or could be, in a somewhat abstract, frenzied circle. What was presented to me looked deliberate and eerie. Selected feathers were aligned in a perfect circle. There was a precision to the way the feathers were placed. The large wing feathers formed the inner ring, smaller feathers comprised the second ring and, finally, the soft, fuzzy tail feathers created a delicate outer ring. All the feathered circles were in perfect order and each feather in a dedicated place of the pattern. The intestines of the bird were at the center of the feathered ring with a broken part of its beak. To the left, just outside of the circled pattern, was one talon.

The presentation of this ceremonious offering looked like a kaleidoscope design, only it was motionless. Even so, I sensed a living presence, or spirit, remained as I looked more closely at the moist, glistening intestines. I was stunned at the theatre of the sight. Did Henry do this? Was there another, perhaps mystical, explanation for the perfection of the design? Was it the creature's last statement of having lived and, if so, what was its message? It was a supernatural event not meant for rationalization.

I will never understand how Henry managed this capture and killing. Yet, I will always remember him courageously dragging his grand prize up the stone steps for me to see. I vividly recall, especially today given Henry is dead, the feel of his soft fur as I scratched his ears and head and the look in his golden-amber eyes when he sat with me that mysterious evening. His gaze was steady and contemplative, and I could almost hear him say, *I did it. I really did it. I am brave, am I not?* Yes, Henry, you were brave.

I stop for food and am, thankfully, keeping it down. However, I continue my mission to reach the cabin tonight. I knew Henry had changed these past months spending more time with me. Was he in pain and I didn't see it? I'll never know now.

You see, no matter where Henry had been or how challenging the hunt, he returned home. His sweetness and gentleness as we sat together on the porch during soft summer rains was a rich experience filled with grace. His indomitable presence and constancy formed our bond. His noble spirit and gentlemanly ways deepened it. And, the essence of our bond endured enough for Henry to come to me in a dream to bid his personal and final farewell. I should not have gone to Maine. I would've been with him. If he were unwell, I would have noticed something. *Perhaps.*

It is midnight as I drive up the long road to the barn. Anna knew I would arrive late and left the lights on in the cabin.

I sit in the car near the barn summoning back a memory just enough to bruise my heartache a bit more. And now that I can no longer stand the pain, I finally see Henry running the five hundred feet of dirt road from the barn to the cabin. Starting with a stealthy feline stride, every muscle at the ready, ears at full attention, he breaks into a lightning-speed sprint with his golden eyes on his prey.

He holds his head high as his spirit soars with the anticipation of the hunt. *Run free with God, dear Henry, for He makes the clouds His chariot and walks upon the wings of the wind.*

October 22

These past days have been spent mourning. I turned off my phones. If anyone knocked on my door, I did not move to open it. The cabin remained dark while I sat on my meditation cushion day and night, trying to calm myself, trying to breathe one painful breath after another. The result was merely more anguish. I knew I was perpetuating my suffering. I berated myself. I demonized everyone I knew so I could hate and curse them. I could not find the inner-strength to obtain equanimity.

I told myself there are many animals in shelters that need homes. But Henry was different. He was part of my soul. He was also part of my life with Dave, for he was the one who knew the woman and brought Henry home teaching me how to train him to be a loyal outdoor cat who would always return to me.

This extreme grief is tied to another significant loss. Dave, too, died here in the pasture raking the horse manure with his tractor. I was in the City, and once again it was Anna who called to tell me that Dave was dead.

When he didn't show up for morning coffee in the village, the group of men he met with daily knew he must still be at my place. They were right. They found him on the ground clutching his chest.

All six horses encircled him. His two border collies lay on each side of his body. You see, the animals he so loved protected him through the night from coyotes, or worse. Dave was sixty-three. Was Henry older than I thought? Maybe six or seven years? Has Dave been gone longer than I realized?

I cry, mourn, rage, and cry again. I drink at night, wake up sick and hung-over. It doesn't take but two or three ounces of vodka in my system now to create a hangover.

I hear knocking again. Is it a dream? Is this a grotesque nightmare? The knocking, this time a loud pounding, resumes. It's probably Anna, but why doesn't she use her key? Yes, I remember now bolting the door and lowering the window blinds. Fists beat on the door. I finally relent and get up, holding my zafu cushion, and open the door. "Arthur! What are you doing here?" I know I look like a zombie. My eyes are swollen shut from crying, only slits remain. My eyelids are bruised and there are hollow dark circles under my eyes from endless weeping. I must look as though I've been beaten by thugs. Arthur said, "Oh my God, what's happened to you, Lee Anne? I was so worried when you didn't answer phone calls or emails. Anna's right behind me with some food." He reached out to take me in his arms, but I slipped to the floor into a fetal position, muttering, "I killed my baby. Lily died too. Dave is dead, and now Henry. I'm all alone." I heard Arthur say, "Anna, Lee Anne's drinking again. There's the vodka. She's just skin and bone." Anna bathed me in a warm bath. Arthur set up the wood stove and brought in stacks of wood and kindling. I was there for four days without heat. I woke a few hours later and heard them in the living room. I got out of bed shaky, but better. I walked into the Great Room, smelling soup, and freshly baked bread.

I wasn't hungry, though. Not yet. I walked over to the vodka bottle and unwound the cap. Anna and Arthur stopped talking. No one can tell an alcoholic not to drink. Overcoming a seductive addiction requires much more than mere human intervention. Assuredly, it is supernatural. Neither Arthur or Anna would know this. I poured it down the drain, then I retrieved another full bottle, and poured that down the sink. Then I looked at the wine bottles stored in a rack. There were several expensive, rare wines I brought back from Maine. I turned to Arthur asking, "Do you want these?" Saying nothing, he rose from the chair and took them out to his car.

"What time is it, Anna?"

"Three o'clock."

"In the morning or afternoon?"

"Afternoon."

I breathed in and exhaled a deep breath for the first time in days.

I sat staring at my desk. In a lifeless voice, I spoke to myself, but out loud, and said, "I need to get to an AA meeting. I've not had anything to drink today. I need a plan. The meetings are in Woodstock and I am not well enough to drive." Arthur was already inside, and said, "I'll drive you, stay in the car through the meeting, or go in with you. Whatever you want. You'll stay at my guest house tonight. Anna said she'll clean up here and prepare for November 1st." Anna added, "I'll pick you up at Arthur's when you feel ready to return home. Okay, sweetie?" I nodded and said I was hungry. They laughed.

"What's November 1st?"

"It's All Saints Day or World Vegan Day. Take your pick. Peddler and I think it would be a good time to spread Henry's ashes around. Are you ready to do that?"

"Yes. But I'd like to do something in the tepee. Okay?"

"Of course. Peddler will handle that. You know Shakespeare has not been around since Peddler saw him watching over Henry. Maybe he'll come back." With that comment, the tears overtook me once again, but I gathered myself and announced, "Let's eat."

Arthur drove me to the meeting and waited outside in his car. I hardly knew anyone in Woodstock, and I was still trembling from the events of the past few days when I walked into the room. A tall man with a mop of brown hair stood up, and I recognized him. A fellow artist. He looked at me and wrapped me in his arms while I sobbed uncontrollably. We sat together, and he held my shaking hands throughout the meeting, especially when it came to my turn to say, "My name is Lee Anne, and I'm an alcoholic."

November 1

This alcoholic experiment was not the first since I started in AA. There were one-night slips here and there, but nothing to the degree of this last experience. And, this must be the last. You will soon know the reasons why. *This must be the last.*

Yet, I've strayed from the story. Or, have I?

I will stay in Arthur's guest house for several days, for I need to be in as many AA meetings possible. I am taking advantage of the warmth and acceptance of AA. No matter how many times one walks out and picks up a drug or drink and returns to the "rooms," there are never questions, repercussions. Just unconditional love and understanding. Our Creator speaks through the wounded, the once-hopeless, the recovered people in the "rooms."

When I first admitted I was an alcoholic eleven years ago, I knew I was predisposed to alcoholism. Today, it is more painful for me to utter these words because if there was the slightest doubt or small hope that maybe I could drink again, I've learned through a harsh reality that I cannot. This is an insidious, demonic habit, and the habit grows stronger even when one stops drinking. I finally proved that for myself.

I return to the cabin today to say goodbye to my beloved feline friend and companion. Peddler set up the wood fire in the tepee creating a glowing and warm welcome for Anna and me. We shared my Assam tea, and Anna sang a Native American song as she smudged with sage and sweet grass. We sat for an hour or so talking about Henry and his beauty and what an old, wise soul he was. I was surprised and delighted when Shakespeare arrived on his preferred limb near the tepee. We got up with Henry's ashes and walked the path to where Peddler found him as Shakespeare flew ahead of us from limb-to-limb. We spread Henry's ashes along the way, and as we approached the spot where he died, we threw the remaining bone dust around the tree. With that, Shakespeare flew three times around the tree where he remained in a steadfast watch over Henry's body the night he went to heaven. He screeched a cry from his soul and flew off. It was the very same wrenching sound I heard that ominous night of the full moon with skeleton trees bending and twisting in a whirlwind when there was no wind. I shiver and know in these fractions of seconds that none of us will see Shakespeare again.

Several gold and silver threads woven into my tapestry are now knotted. Their stories have ended. Never their memories.

2005

As far as the east is from the west, so far does He remove our transgressions from us.

~Psalm 103:12

August 15

Following Henry's memorial, I spent these many months devoting myself to the studio and all the photos I amassed during my time in Maine. I wrote little-to-nothing on the story promised to you, other than notations of facts and memories as they surfaced. And, I decided to take gallery space in the village after all.

Arthur and I spent more time together as well. Our focus was the firm. How well, or not, it was doing regarding existing clients and increased business. And, it was not doing well.

Apparently, most consulting firms were experiencing a downturn in revenue due to fewer consulting assignments. I was no longer a partner in the firm, but I certainly did not want to see its demise either. Arthur assured me we were not at that point, but we needed to downsize our staff as well as our fees. The marketplace would no longer support premium-pricing for our services.

I sensed the business was shrinking, but Arthur kept it afloat, and I handled what I could in assignments. He assessed the financial investments marketers made in their agencies for advertising, which was in the millions-to-billions of dollars depending on the size of the client. I worked with softer data, assessing the client and agency relationship, their ability to effectively communicate with one another not only within their own organization, but with their agency partners. All our work was for the benefit of a better creative product, building a healthy, wealthy brand. We brought these two aspects of hard and soft data together under the umbrella of a proprietary ROI formula, the marketer's ROI value-for-investment in its agency. We pioneered the process, adopted by many who followed us.

Arthur stopped by to see me today to ask about my financial statements. I found that odd and told him I didn't know for I rarely looked at them. He asked to see the latest. And, therein was the shock. My $1,000,000 portfolio lost half its worth in late 2001 when there was a sizeable dip in the market. Moreover, I was also draining the remaining funds using a unique non-taxable federal offering at that time. The rude awakening was that my retirement funds shrunk to $150,000 as of the July 2005 statement. Arthur was livid with our broker, for the broker was to have mirrored whatever Arthur did in investment and divestment for my portfolio as well. Arthur knew I would never give attention to it, so he rightfully gave those instructions. Our broker did not follow Arthur's program and offered his own ideas instead. I thought they were great, not understanding how naïve and fatally ignorant I was about the stock market.

Still, we had fees coming in, although my given assignments were small, and based on what Arthur told me, they would shrink further. My upkeep, however, was substantial between the cabin and the gallery. He was not panicked and asked me to have faith in the universe. It would all work out. I was less optimistic. I could feel a change coming. The darkness that stalked me for years had arrived. And, it had a firm grip on my heart and soul. I am grateful now that I had no idea of the magnitude or nature of this black abyss.

August 16

Though the financial news was devastating, I had no time to process it. For at this moment, on this day, it was easy to put aside the whole issue. I received an urgent phone call early this morning. My father is dying.

I made quick arrangements to fly into Ft. Lauderdale. I was expecting to visit dad in his bed hooked up to machines and tubes. This was not the case for he rallied during my travel time. He said, "This is not my time." And, he was right.

Instead, my father, ninety-three years old, sits in a wheelchair with a thin left leg crossed over the right and his arms folded. He looks small. My stepmother stands close to him at the ready to help should he need it. As I enter the building housing the infirm and aging, I register little. I only see my dad's clear blue eyes unclouded by age retaining an intensity of spirit and purpose I had never seen before.

Our eyes lock into one another's. Through them, for a few suspended moments, we have an immediate understanding, an unspoken communication. *We made our journey. Through it all, we accomplished what we needed to do. We did our best. We understand more. And, we love more.* Then, spiraling back into the presence of others, I move towards him with my arms outstretched. Like a great Samurai warrior wounded in his final battle, his honor refusing to give way to frailty, my father stands to greet me, bracing himself on trembling arms and hands and unsteady limbs. I was amazed at the nobility and courage of this act as I carefully embrace his fragile frame and kiss his cool cheek. I feel his thin skin and sharp bones, for this once strapping one-hundred-and-eighty-pound man who fought blazing fires in Cleveland, Ohio, now weighed one-hundred-and-ten pounds. Proudly, he sits down as he stood moments before, shaking and unsteady, but without anyone's help.

Though his body was tired and worn from old age, his mind remained clear, and his focus was keen like that of a great white wolf ever alert observing, listening, taking it all in, missing nothing, seeing everything.

As I sit next to him and take his hand, I notice the gossamer-like skin covering his bones. We sit silently for a few moments looking at one another. I observe how long and slender his fingers are as his hands gracefully draped over the arms of his chair. These are the hands of an artist or should have been, for they are exceedingly graceful. I never looked closely at his hands before. I regret not having my camera. A photographer always carries a camera. I could have photographed his delicate, slender hands, but perhaps the image was one not to be captured other than in my mind's eye to remember. I did not know then that this was the last time I would see my father.

A willingness to acknowledge my father's genuine essence, though painful at times, was a revelation. Wisdom, rather than malice, is borne amidst pain. My dad was neither famous nor infamous, yet he paid attention to the small, humble acts of daily life. He provided a lifetime of service to many people. He provided the basic needs of his family under challenging, painful circumstances. He gave of himself to all eight of his brothers, sisters, respective spouses, and mothers-in-law during their illnesses as most passed away over the many decades that he lived. He was a courageous man who walked into raging fires to rescue others, which he never spoke of. I recall nights he arrived home exhausted covered in soot and red-faced from a severe fire. I called him when 9/11 occurred and tried to elicit some comments from him about the 'first responders.' He was overwhelmed, choking back tears, and in a scratchy voice said, "Please don't ask me anything. It brings back nightmares."

The uncompromising truth, however, the marrow of our existence together, is that my father did not want a child. It no longer hurts, for I believe, I must believe, that once I entered his world, he loved me as best he could. I do not know how our love would be defined, but there was love between us.

I pray that dad is free from his bondages. The quick anger he wore on his face and held in his heart, the pain and guilt of his internal world, and prejudices towards others whom he did not know, nor even tried to understand. I wept a little when dad died. Now as I write, I find, in truth, I do not know if I miss him. At times something within me cries out for my father. At other times, I'm reminded of advice he provided. As if he's whispering now, I hear his words both painful and clear. *Always save your money.*

I developed compassion and forgiveness for dad. I am alive, and my life is rich with good memories he helped create. After all, he did forge my birth certificate, give in to my wishes to dance and leave high school, and encouraged me to be an independent woman. Dad always said, "Never depend on anyone else to take care of you, not even a husband. Always find a way to manage your own life."

My father was a brave man. Brave enough to admit a gritty, heartbreaking truth to his only daughter on a rainy October afternoon surrounded by the falling leaves on Thirty-Third Street in New York City.

Dad passed away one year later just short of his ninety-fourth birthday. I know he wanted to live to be one hundred. Sorry dad. Ninety-four is not bad. Not bad at all.

November 7

The visit with my dad, the loss of Henry, financial stress took their emotional toll on me, so I've not written one page since I saw my father. I am relieved to be at my desk once again. But as dawn breaks, my heart can't help but fill with memories of Henry. I have not sought another furry, four-legged companion. It is not time.

I mourn many things and I find the struggle to stay afloat financially stressful and, at times, sheer anguish. Anna tries to comfort me and teach me how to live simply, frugally, but I still have hope that money will materialize.

As the years progress, the threads eventually weave themselves into each life tapestry, and then the work should be complete yet mine remains unfinished. What I need to do most is to write the final piece of the story so I can rest knowing I have recorded all the details. All the truths.

My mother killed herself on St. Valentine's Day, 1971. She swallowed a fifth of cheap scotch with a bottle of tranquilizers and another bottle of digitalis. She was fifty-three years old and died alone in the upper West Side apartment in New York City that we once shared during my performing arts career.

I finally forgave my father but forgiving my mother happened years before. I was well on my way to becoming exactly like her; depressed, alcoholic, crazed.

My mother's anguish and rage prevailed for the twenty-eight years I knew her. For years after her suicide, I often thought about my sad, beautiful mother with her dark bedroom eyes, sensual laugh, and anger that shredded the souls of others. What I discovered traveling into this abyss eventually changed the size of my heart.

On my fiftieth birthday, sober for ninety-days, I encountered her unexpectedly through a long meditation. During the meditation, I saw a perfectly shaped pulsating pink heart rimmed with an indigo blue light. Tiny drops of blood fell from the center of the heart with each beat. I knew it was my mother's heart. I sensed her presence along with a faint scent of Shalimar. I literally felt her deep, endless sadness too. I physically absorbed her pain and remorse not only from those years I knew her as her daughter but all the years of her life of which I knew nothing. Then I saw her. She was lovely. Tall and slender with curly short bobbed hair. Her skin was lighter than the olive-skinned mother I knew. We strolled under a blue sky in a meadow with wildflowers and blue-green grass. I did not try to touch her for instinct told me it was not possible. The slender grasses swayed with a soft, warm breeze as she stood there with tears in her eyes asking, "Are you happy? Are you well?" I replied, "Yes, mom. I am happy, creative, and now that I'm sober, life is even better." She asked, "How is your relationship with God?" I was surprised and answered feebly, "It's okay I guess. Why?" She looked at me with her brown eyes, now softened with kindness I never saw, and said, "The Lord should be the most important being in your life. I sense He is not." Her tone did not condemn me, but there was a note of genuine concern. I did not understand her comment, and, therefore, dismissed it.

I told her how much I missed her, that I no longer blamed her for her behaviors and anger, and that I longed to have just one more long conversation, one in which we could crystallize the joys and absolve the sorrows of our life together. She nodded saying, "All is well, and all will be well. We will do this, but not this day." She smiled, reaching out to touch me but did not, then turned and walked further away into a grove of olive trees until I no longer saw her or sensed her presence. I emerged from the meditation with a firm conviction that my mother had visited me. Was this imagination, or an actual mystical experience? I don't believe proving it, or not, is relevant.

I gave superficial thought to what she meant concerning my relationship with God. I was, indeed, dealing with God in my life due to my new sobriety in AA. God is the Higher Power in the "rooms." Surrendering to a power greater than ourselves is embedded in the first three Steps of the Program. *For it is God who works in you to will and to act to fulfill His good purpose.* Yes, it's hard work to humble oneself to honor God in the Steps. Even so, I chose not to focus on her probing questions regarding God. It didn't occur to me that she might have first-hand experience. All I cared about was that the occurrence, however I characterized it, allowed me to release the past and open my heart to understanding and compassion and forgiveness. Crusty barnacles clinging to my heart dropped away leaving a dwelling place for at least some love to venture in.

With that "visitation" and my AA meetings, I presumed I had closure. I was incorrect. Life had more lessons for me.

A few days following the meditation, I stepped into a hidden hole in the grass leading to the barn. I broke my right ankle and was bound to a wheelchair. I was, for the most part, immobile once again. I, who still moved like a dancer and filled my days with cameras, tripod, lenses or easel, paintbrushes and oils to bring a vision to life, believed I was unable to do any of these things.

When the accident first occurred, I crumbled emotionally and spiritually. I cried and raged at myself and at the world and at God. The long since forgotten polio, its encumbrances, physical pain, and entrapment of my body, rolled over me like a tsunami. The black hole of my mother's madness asserted itself. My art studio stood fallow. I no longer smelled the oil paint and wax, while standing at the slop sink carefully cleaning my brushes after a long, productive painting session. I could not spontaneously grab my camera to capture an image I knew would not pass my way again. All was lost. Forever.

This was my mother's darkness, her Shalimar, her complete loss of spirit. I was in this depressive state for three days, and during those days I watched and listened to the persistent rain. Someone, somewhere once said it takes three days for the world to turn upside down and three days for it to turn right side up. After the three days of rain, I felt a slight stirring within. The darkness slowly lifted as I began to see that the showers heralded a christening of the land as well as a cleansing of my spirit. My artist's eye eventually returned after sitting for hours in the wheelchair really seeing, genuinely hearing the steady rain.

The rain finally passed, and in its place, flirtatious streaks of sunshine broke through dark clouds giving new life to my wheel-chair-view of the world with a pair of white butterflies that never entirely left one another in their pas de deux from flower to bush to tree limb.

The weeks of confinement ahead became unimportant, for I realized I could still capture my images through words. I wrote poems, short stories, and long essays about life, nature, and, yes, my feelings about God too.

My broken ankle and confinement were blessings. The attachment to my creative activity held the similar import my mother attached to her one-ounce bottle of Shalimar. Work defined me.

Shalimar was aspirational for her. I clearly, and finally, understood what she felt. I was awed by the bottomless pit to which I almost surrendered, for I believed at the time that I was gently touched by my mother's madness.

Through forgiveness, my heart finally opened, even absorbed, my mother's pain. Since that day, I never blamed her again or berated her for an unwelcome circumstance in my life. Importantly, her greatest legacy to me was to be witness to how her innate creativity was severely repressed. I made choices in my life so that I could nurture my artistic endeavors, fully engaging my imagination. Mom did not know how to do this for herself, nor did anyone encourage her.

There is a one-ounce Baccarat crystal bottle of Shalimar perfume sitting on my bathroom vanity. A bottle always resides with me and every so often I dab the sweet essence behind my ears and on my wrists, a modest gesture and a gentle bow of tribute to my mother's life. For many years now on St. Valentine's Day, I purchase a dozen roses to honor her and our time together on the Blue Highways. I know no one else remembers her, or cares to, so my action is not only one of forgiveness, but of deep, genuine love.

I think of my sister, Lily, and our short time together in the womb of our mother and her tiny life force ending in violence. Our parents were mere humans. Flawed, filled with fear and guilt. Even though they prayed, they lacked a depth of faith, and, therefore, wisdom. I see now how my heart was hardened when I insisted on traveling at the risk of losing the only child I had a chance of bringing into this world. And I too lacked trust and faith and wisdom.

At sixty-two, I do feel an emptiness of not having children, a robust family with grandchildren too. Yet I have given birth to many images and thousands of words and mentored younger women and men over the years. Maybe there is some merit in these small things.

I sit in the single chair on the studio balcony. A bald-eagle glides over bare treetops and cloud-capped mountains. A slow, ceaseless rain drips from the studio gutter onto an empty cedar bench below. A bird's hosanna soars in purity as it circles dry places. A silver fox stops on its trek to somewhere and stares up at me. We lock gazes. He moves on. I stay. The bench remains empty, but my eyes are full for they have been walked upon.

The experience is an omen.

2018 Reprise

You have turned for me my mourning into dancing;
You have loosed my sackcloth and clothed me with gladness,
that my glory may sing Your praise and not be silent.
O Lord my God, I will give thanks to You forever!

~ Psalm 30:11-12

January 17

Thirteen years have passed since I saw the silver fox. I believe he was an omen and not a happy one. BEWARE! THERE ARE STORMY SEAS AHEAD. What happened to my story? It was complete in what I believed was the whole story. There was closure in forgiveness, love, joy, sorrow, truths revealed, lives lived and lives lost. I believed it was time to write THE END and I did. I set it aside in my desk's center drawer contemplating from time-to-time if indeed I would ever publish it. I resume the narrative thirteen years later for how could I possibly know then what was to unfold?

My gallery limped along. While our consulting firm did well for Arthur, it did not work for me. All the consulting assignments were investment focused. There were no longer projects requiring my skills in relationship management.

I struggled financially to keep the cabin and gallery afloat. I spent my days and evenings at the gallery. However, a point in time was reached when I no longer had enough income to support both my cabin and gallery. I finally secured a sizeable home equity loan on what was a mortgage-free property.

Financial matters limped along until 2008. Everything stopped with the Great Recession. It not only came to a halt for me but for hundreds of thousands of people. Arthur downsized the firm, sold our Chelsea loft-offices in New York City, and moved to his property in upstate New York, resuming the consulting practice in this beautiful region of the Hudson Valley. He was liquid when the Great Recession lowered itself upon our lives because he was prudent with the care of his investment portfolio, surviving better than most.

I had no portfolio left. I was trying to live on my social security but was unsuccessful due to my overhead costs and house debt. I was confronted with the next loss in my life. My gallery shuttered its doors December 31st, 2008.

I just barely managed to maintain the costs of the cabin for several more years and did so with the sale of some art to collectors and a few modest assignments writing proposals and final reports for Arthur. None of it was enough, though, for I was under water. I was bankrupt.

Bankruptcy is mortifying to most, and it was for me except I needed to treat it as merely another hurdle to surmount. There was no time to flagellate myself, indulge in self-pity or remorse. I needed a plan to survive and to execute it with my dignity intact.

Nonetheless, the haunting fear following me these many years was actualized. I lost my cabin, my sanctuary, bringing my season of life in Camelot to a demoralizing end.

The bank began foreclosure proceedings on the cabin property as they were doing with thousands of homes. I was not alone, but still, it was my nightmare. Nothing that happened was remotely close to my expectations. It is one thing to hope, for hope is good. It is another to form expectations. Life unfolds in ways that defy assumptions.

The Bible says, *if riches increase, do not set your heart upon them.* I framed my life around materialism and the ability to earn money, and even more money as I needed it. Money was my god, and I was its slave.

I must stop for now and revisit this tomorrow. An Arctic blast has descended upon us with fierce and disturbingly persistent winds. The windows rattle while the wood stoves need attention. Moreover, I need more reflection to write the truth about the deterioration of my tapestry, my life.

January 18

5:30 A.M.—I am completely isolated from the world. There must be nine feet of snow! The outdoor lights are still on yet I barely see the top of my truck. Thankfully, there has been no power outage. Yet. My auto-generator broke and I haven't the money to repair it.

7:30 A.M.—Daylight arrives and unveils a winter wonderland, though I have no desire to photograph the pristine beauty outside my window. I am alone and lonely. Anna is away for a few weeks, and Peddler always goes south in the winter to see his woman friend in some mysterious place he's never disclosed. So, I drink tea and write nonstop.

After the bankruptcy, the little material wealth I still possessed evaporated. Everything. Even the small fees from free-lance consulting. I sold all my designer clothing, Baccarat crystal stemware, hand-forged James Robinson silver flatware, one-of-a-kind jewelry and custom-made clothes, artwork, cameras, lenses, and all my painting supplies. I auctioned my antique furniture, fur coats and jackets, Royal Copenhagen porcelain dinner ware, rare English tea sets, and so much more. All acquired when money flowed.

I did not know how, or where I could live on my social security. I launched a marketing campaign in upstate New York highlighting my business and creative skills. Résumés and letters were mailed, advertisements were placed, and I made warm and cold calls to people and places I knew and did not know. There was not one inquiry over many months.

As the bank marched on with its foreclosure, I soldiered on hunting for a room, a small apartment, perhaps a caretaker's cottage. But my efforts brought no results. I was desperate and felt my greatest fear materializing with each new day and moment—being left without anything or anyone. I was online seeking apartment rentals in the four-hundred-dollar range when an ad for senior subsidized housing popped up on my screen. I didn't know anything about subsidized housing but pursued it. A major problem was solved presenting me with a safe, clean, and quiet apartment I could afford.

Friends, acquaintances, and others who were long absent in my life surfaced from known as well as surprising places. They helped me pack and move the remaining elements of my life from my mountaintop cabin and barn studio to a modest apartment and a new chapter in my life.

March 14

 The big move, the sale of so many treasured items and gifting to others, was over. Anna helped me put a few small personal boxes and suitcases into my new wheels, a slightly rusted six-year-old Honda Fit. I had no more credit, so I sold my fully loaded Ford 150 truck, and paid cash for a blue-lavender car with decent mileage.

 I drove down the long dirt road I once drove up with such anticipation and wonderment. The curtain had already fallen on that scene, so I did not look back. I chose instead to remember the years in Camelot—living a rare and beautiful life at the cabin. Watching Henry sleep, hunt, and run. Stacking wood and feeding the wood stoves. Loving Dave. Galloping on a horse named Bubba. Walks in pristine snow that crunched with each step. Gazing up at brilliant start-studded skies. Ceremonies of joy and sorrow in the tepee. And one barred owl I named Shakespeare.

March 27

Subsidized apartments are a haven for the elderly, or disabled, who fiercely strive to maintain their independence. While I admire their efforts, at first the building appeared to be a nursing home as I walked through the lobby past the walkers, wheelchairs, canes, and people whose lives rarely extended beyond this small village. I had nothing in common with my neighbors except that none of us had the money to live in our own homes or rent something at full market rates. I eventually came to a more compassionate view of the courage my neighbors have and how they face each new challenge and reality of aging. They are an inspiration. Sadly, for me, I averted everyone in the beginning.

During my first three months in this apartment, I cried most of the time. I was overcome with depression and suicidal thoughts while trying to continue the writing of my story. So, I stopped. One afternoon I wailed with grief. I mourned all I believed I lost. There were no close friends I could turn to who would truly understand. I blamed God most of all. *What did I do to deserve this?* However, I soon learned that contrary to secular and some conservative Christian beliefs, God does not punish. He "allows" trials in our lives *but works all things for the good for those who believe.*

I explored various therapeutic modalities through the years. Psychiatrists and unique therapies like 'rebirthing.' I turned to "religion" several times including Catholicism and then Episcopalian churches for several years. As you may recall, I called myself a Christian-Buddhist for a short time. Finally, I was gently brought to an evangelical church. I thought as a progressive liberal I was mismatched for the latter and, oh, I most certainly was! Also, I did not believe that the Bible was the literal Word of God. Yet, *yet,* something inside urged me to study and not just demean the Bible for the sake of critique and a false sense of intellectual superiority. I learned more about its historical development, the importance of context, who was speaking to whom at what time, and the teachings of Jesus, the radical, loving, compassionate teachings of Jesus. I discovered they were invaluable, but I was wary of the extremists, the alternative-right politically, so I studied more. I read the writings of C.S. Lewis and G.K. Chesterton who said, *"The Christian ideal has not been tried and found wanting. It has been found difficult; and left untried."* I listened to a variety of educated theologians and pastors unwrap the complexities, subtleties, and teachings of God's Word with focus, application of the lessons, and their own love of Jesus. I spent hours online watching and listening to intellectual and heated debates among Christian and atheist scholars as well as apologists for Christ, chief among them, Ravi Zacharias.

I decided I could figure this out for myself. I was smug, arrogant, and filled with pride. After all, what was I doing in subsidized housing with people about to die? How did I reach the depth of needing to apply for Food Stamps? The Biblical teachings pulled and tugged at my heart while I remained stubborn. The deity of my "I" prevailed. I could. I would. I can. The "I" was all pervasive. The same "I" that landed me in this situation! The "I" in my life that spent money, bought unnecessary material stuff and things, the "I" that never gave credit to God for the good fortune I enjoyed, my sobriety, my talents, and prevailing good health, especially in these mature years. When these insights tumbled on to me, the walls of my apartment, my utter aloneness in the world, the continuing mourning of everything I lost enveloped my soul as I literally believed I was a broken, useless, and selfish creature for most of my life. Though I did not drink through these upheavals, the feelings were not unlike hitting an alcoholic bottom. I was knocked down for the full count. It was unequivocal spiritual deprivation. And it was humbling. As I look back now, the LORD had me exactly where He wanted me. Broken in spirit with a contrite heart. His joy comes when He saves His children and makes them whole again with renewed hearts and minds.

I reluctantly kneeled in the center of my living room floor uttering words I thought I would never say. *Dear God, I am done. I can't do it anymore. I've been the center of my universe from birth. I have sinned in ways I do not even understand yet I know that it is so. I have lied. I have belittled people. I am ungrateful. I have shown no compassion except to those close to me. Jesus, You speak of love in Your teachings. I don't know that I ever loved in the way You intend it. I don't love now. I feel silly, a simple fool here on my knees, but I don't want to die. I don't. I want to live. I want to give back. I want to love. Please, dear Jesus, come into my heart and use me for Your will. Give me the chance to use Your gifts to me for Your will and not mine. I am so sorry. Forgive me. I am so very sorry. I want to glorify You in all that I say, in all that I do, and with all that I have.*

Tears streamed down my cheeks while my breathing slowed and my freezing body warmed again. I wish I could present a dramatic accounting of what happened in the immediate moments following my Sinner's Prayer. There was no bright light filling the room, nor did I hear a thundering voice. However, an inexplicable peace washed over me. A longing was lifted from my heart, mind, and thirsty soul. Jesus said, *Take my yoke upon you, and learn from me, for I am gentle and lowly in heart, and you will find rest for your souls.*

For my yoke is easy, and my burden is light. Nevertheless, I still did not trust this serenity to last and, of course, the rational part of my brain reduced the experience to a cathartic event.

However, it did last in varying degrees. My heart slowly softened filling with a little more love and then a little more as time went on. My mind too started seeing the world through a different moral lens. I was drawn once again to Bible-based teachings and a Christ-focused church I once attended. Walking in the footsteps of Christ is the most challenging, frustrating, and joyful journey I've embarked upon. It requires the utmost surrender of our external life so that little, if anything, of the worldly-world appeals to the disciple that does not appeal to Him. Yet the materialistic things of the flesh are only the beginning. A genuine humility is required for a follower to yield to His Will rather than her own. As the years progressed, I read God's Word breathed into the Bible, and they ultimately awakened on the page as living and dancing poetic energy. Another layer of burden was lifted. I grew in my walk with Christ, albeit sometimes kicking and screaming and doubting. Today, *I know that I know that I know*—who I am in Christ and how much He loves me.

For one who has never experienced His presence in a personal relationship, I understand that my position is puzzling for a wholly pragmatic mind to absorb. Yet I walk and talk with Him all the time while living each precious day of life. I would not have it, nor could I have it, any other way. He is my Lord and my Friend. Jesus *is* the center of my life.

Loving God, you see, is an affair of the heart.

March 31

My morning rituals have not changed too much in my apartment from life at the cabin. I still rise early and brew Assam tea. Before writing starts, however, I now pray and read scripture or writings related to the Bible and its teachings.

After all the wailing and moaning about where I live, I must confess that my apartment is a comfortable and pretty one-bedroom filled with light. It dwells in the charming historic Village of Athens, New York situated along the Hudson River. The views from each of my four windows are of woodlands and wildlife. Indeed, it is more like a tree-house apartment, but also, a safe harbor, and a place I finally call home.

There is a blizzard raging outside, and for the first time in years, there's nothing for me to do. The plows will come and clear away our paths and the parking lot. Our cars will be cleaned off, and all will be done. But I watch the snow, its bluster and beauty, as it accumulates to several inches on the trees' limbs and branches outside my windows. To my delight, there is suddenly a profusion of birds. Woodpeckers, chickadees, bluebirds with fluffy white beards, many, many cardinals, doves, and blackbirds, all flying so fast that I wonder if I can capture them with my camera through my windows. My hand reaches for the one remaining camera, unused too long, and I begin taking pictures for the balance of the morning.

What beauty and miracles of Creation these are! After most of the birds find shelter, one bright crimson cardinal remains in the purity of the sinless snow. I take the picture of his perfection. To my amazement, each picture sings to me. I realize how little I have to do with the birth of these delightful images. I am merely the mechanic behind the camera. I have always been His instrument from the phenomenon of my birth to the day the brace broke away from my leg revealing a gift to dance. This talent, this gift, led me onto paths opening worlds I could not dream would happen in my life. I cannot conceive how I ever thought I did it myself. Oh yes. I belong to Him.

August 27

The story ends. Soon. I started this narrative on this day and dismissed the fact that it was my seventy-fifth birthday. The open book on my lap is a well-worn Bible. Yes, in our culture I am considered old. I note a visible decline in my face, especially my body, but remain in excellent health. While my body still moves for which I thank the Lord each day, it is with greater frequency becoming a battleground. Years of dance injuries in an era when these were rarely tended to with physical therapists have come to collect their dues. Even so, I take my daily walks, no longer with the snake stick for I gave it to Anna to return to Peddler should he return some day. I climb steep roadways but take the hills with a steady, respectful rhythm, and do ballet stretches. I've come to accept the measured pace of age as each decade brings its new lessons for us to embrace.

It is said that aging is a loss of youth, vitality, health and, sadly, dignity for some. True and not true. It is how we perceive this process. Is it loss or gain? I clearly see that the valleys into which I fell and the mountains I climbed toward redemption, were touchstones, vital life teachings at each bend, twist, and turn of this earthly sojourn.

A peaceful journey into the unavoidable experiences of aging, mourning loss of spouses, friends, children, beloved pets, and yet continuing to long for youth, freedom from pain, and more, demands an unalterable acceptance of what is now. Just now. Think about the future and one runs the risk of making an unholy alliance with depression and fear. Longing for the past and one faces the same demons.

Our country's cultural values do not hold in high esteem the dignity inherent in aging, the wisdom acquired, the beauty in a wrinkled face, graying hair, or the body shifting downward. We are impermanent creatures as everything is. We will all die. *As for mortals, our days are like a flower of the field, and we flourish. When the wind passes over it, we are no more, and the place where we bloomed no longer knows us.* The aches, pains, stiffness, are the early announcements. Yet how grateful I am to have lived long enough to joyfully look forward to each new day.

I sit with my Bible reading, underscoring verses to make notes, and look up to see dawn's light slip into view through lush woodland trees bringing slivers of colors to the sky composed of gold and pink and purple. Amber leaves, like giant snowflakes, already fall as I hear them come to rest on the forest floor.

I sit at a desk that is now my studio, all six by eight feet of it. And, there is someone else with me. Her name is Abbey. She is now five years old. A Basic Model Tabby 101. Her story is special as is the case with all rescue animals.

She was discovered on the roadside giving birth to several kittens. A couple saw this event, scooped her and the kittens up in their jackets, and rushed them to the nearest vet. All her kittens were born and soon adopted. Only Abbey was left in the adoption center at PetSmart. I walked towards the back of the store where the cats were housed. I was ready. After several months in the apartment, I finally missed the second heartbeat in my home.

I saw her staring at me. Her eyes followed me no matter where I walked, admiring all the cats, mostly young kittens. I decided to inquire about this feline who continued to stare at me. They released her from the cage, told her story, while she walked straight to me, jumped into my lap, and fell asleep with a loud purr. Without doubt, she claimed me as her new human mother. Abbey is safe now, never goes outside, and knows she is loved.

While I drink my tea and write, Abbey takes a different position than did Henry. She sleeps behind my computer. She has four window sills she travels to each day several times a day to observe the abundance of birds, squirrels, chipmunks, deer, wild turkey, and other cats.

There was a choir of birds singing robustly this morning, and then they faded away. All but one. A large, big-breasted, bright crimson cardinal sat on the closest limb of the closest tree to my desk's window. Could this be the very same one from winter? He sang, without pause, for a half-hour or more! I took pictures as he continued with his song. *Who are you?* He sang a little while longer and then flew off. Ah! How magnificent. What a perfect birthday greeting.

Though seventy-five years is a milestone, there is no grand celebration planned. I will deliver meals to some homebound people and then go to my friend's house for tea and chocolate. Later, I'm having dinner with my first AA sponsor. I know Anna will call, Arthur called yesterday from his home in Switzerland, and Peddler moved away to a place unknown to us.

Gifts of grace and abundance abound in my life. I am blessed with birdsong upon waking every morning, and summer fire-flies that light-up like miniature lanterns at night. My walks take me through the Village to the magnificent Hudson River where morning mists lift off the water, or a rainbow hovers long enough for my camera to capture the marvel. I watch the River's waters flow one way and then another, and in the winter the ice flows are stunning, carved blocks floating, melting, refreezing and then, they are gone with the arrival of spring. I am surrounded by good, neighborly people who actually say and mean *good morning*.

And now the time has come to finish my story.

At one stage in the materialistic worldview, I had it all. *All* meaning a fair amount of money, beautiful clothes, a loft apartment in the West Village of New York City, and a storybook log cabin on top of a mountain.

When I look back, I ask what happened? Life-choices were made while I was dead-in-the-spirit, turning away from God rather than running to Him. Over a decade-and-a-half, I watched my financial status move from very-comfortable-to-scarcity. I blame no one, and no longer myself, the latter requiring I forgive myself as God did and move forward.

I felt outside of time surrendering to each trial as it occurred. I sensed, as I always had that I was protected. For two decades, the restlessness I felt was the STILL SMALL VOICE urging me to simplify my life. Surely, when I walked into my first AA meeting, the calm, sweet voice guided me there. When I look upon the weaving of my life tapestry, I now know that God has been weaving the cloth, not I, and He is *not* unraveling it but improving it for whatever time is left to me. God saved my life at birth in my mother's womb. How was it possible to survive an abortion and blood poisoning without supernatural intervention? He saved me again from polio and epilepsy, and later in life from the devastation of alcohol. He helped me to forgive and love a mother and father who did not, and could not, love due to their own pain.

In hindsight, all the events, every single one in my life, were woven together to bring me out of bondage into freedom—freedom of ease and peace from the world's clamor and clutter and things. Though I did not hear His voice for years, I listen to Him now. I try not to miss even a whisper of His guidance and love.

Do I miss any of it? No. What I have is simple. For the moment, I've lost the passion for photographing one more flower or tree. I know I will use my camera again, as I did for the birds, yet I sense it may be for very different subjects. Or, not. It's His guidance I follow. Not mine. My writing continues, though, and I do not stop.

When I lost my cabin home, I didn't know what the next day would bring, or what I was going to do. In these quiet seasons of contemplation and writing, a revelation emerged. I have serious work ahead: Learning to love more, being a better human example on this planet, and serving wherever, and however, I am able. Loving and serving Him is why I was born.

Having it all and losing it helped me to discover what is most important. My wealth today is not measurable by worldly standards, for my annual income is below the poverty level. And yet, I am grateful for the prosperity in my life. I understand Anna and Peddler now and what they were trying to teach me.

Writing and creating art was once essential for me to live, and they remain so but for a different reason. These are gifts given to me when I was born. I must use them up for Him. My words and images can be meaningful contributions toward helping and serving others, or just one person. Who would have thought that a child nearly-never-born would be here today to tell her story? What I learned throughout the writing of these pages is at the genesis of my account. There are paths we choose and others we must take. There are truths and wounds we need to face and walk into with courage, like Daniel into the furnace-fire. We cannot avoid that life is unbearably beautiful, with crevices and rocks, clear lakes and open meadows, and, yes, those deep valleys to descend and high mountains to climb.

Two months ago I learned that a land developer bought my cabin property, so I drove to my old homestead to see what it looked like. They carved up the mountain terrain, meadows, and walking trails, leaving instead decimated forest land. The old hemlock trees were felled. There were too many homes and people and noise for wildlife to remain.

This is a ruinous loss of purity in a place where God showed His face. They erased the energy of a horse named Bubba who galloped over unfettered roads and meadows. And now, only I will know the essence of a unique owl, Shakespeare, and a well-loved feline companion named Henry. Perhaps, *just perhaps,* there are echoes of footsteps from Dave, Anna, Peddler, Henry, and me. Do the distinctive calls of Shakespeare and coyotes reverberate too? And, is there any spirit-of-life left in the mountain to remember us?

Driving back to my little Village on the Hudson River, I felt a mixed blessing was bestowed upon me. While sad, I found I was grateful for the loss of Camelot. God really does know what to do and when for He sees what we cannot. I could not have remained in Camelot as the worldly-world took it over for its greedy pleasure and destruction. *They desecrated sacred ground.* I would have been in prison rather than a sanctuary.

My story is complete. However, not the tapestry of my life, or my work. I continue to write and my camera stands ready when I choose to pick it up again. I paint with abandonment for the sheer joy of it. These are my daily tasks I am grateful to do. They are the music of the heart and the dance of my soul. The Lord is my constant companion. There is rarely a decision I make, an action taken, a word said, without checking with my Friend.

And, with these final words, the crimson cardinal returns and sings again! I've named him Isaiah. He is talkative as well as musical and filled with a constancy of joy. I can't help but think of some of the inspiring lyrics from a worship song by Hillsong: *And as You speak a hundred billion galaxies are born. In the vapor of Your breath the planets form. If the stars were made to worship so will I.* In an interview with one of Hillsong's lead singers, he spoke about the inspiration of God as Artist/Creator and how the lyrics flowed from that revelation. I open the window screen and place five unsalted peanuts on the windowsill. Following Isaiah's songs-of-praise, he flies to the window five times to take each peanut back to his mate. He flies one more time to the open window fluttering his wings while looking at me. I'm astonished for his crimson wings are spread wide and close enough for me to touch. I reach for the camera, but the Creator says *no*. I feel my hand is literally held back. Ah, yes, this is a birthday blessing for me alone.

You see, Isaiah is quite remarkable. And as he sings His praises, *so will I.*

Selah

Acknowledgements

God has been my co-Creator for the two decades it took me to write this small volume. He worked through people including some tough critics, encouraging friends, tender-but-firm copy editors, and those who simply cared enough to read through the many iterations I provided through the years. Their names follow with my deepest gratitude: Christine La Bella, Pauline Erickson, Zuzonna Huot, Carol Fountain, Janet Sanders, Keith Mueller, Joe Stefko, Arthur Anderson, Don Paczkowski, and April Martin. A special thank you to Pastor Craig Paczkowski for taking gentle care in the reading and blessing of this little book. Finally, I shower abundant kudos upon Elizabeth Cline who designed the book from cover-to-cover and without whom this volume would not be in your hands.

My love to each of you *always* in His name.

Made in the USA
Middletown, DE
04 June 2019